THIS
IS
WHERE
I
STAND

Other Books by
Rue Anne Hass, M.A.

Opening the Cage of Pain with EFT:
Let Your Spirit Fly Free
(available in English and Spanish)

The Discovery Book
EFT and the 8 Master Keys

The 8 Master Keys to Healing What Hurts
For the Highly Sensitive Person

THIS
IS
WHERE
I
STAND

Rue Anne Hass, M.A.

ISBN: 978-0-9791700-4-1

THIS IS WHERE I STAND

Rue Hass: IntuitiveMentoring.com

Book Design by Angela Treat Lyon

References:
Gary Craig's comprehensive website: EmoFree.com
Dr. Patricia Carrington: EFTupdate.com
Resources: EFTBooks.com for Books, Tele-Classes,
Audios, CDs, DVDs and other EFT materials

Unbounded gratitude to Gary Craig for EFT,
and to Dr. Patricia Carrington for her
brilliant addition of the Choices Method

Published by: **Starseed Publications**
2204 E Grand Ave., Everett, WA 98201

Second Edition: August 2008

Printed in the United States of America
8 7 6 5 4 3 2 1 0 9

CONTENTS

All names of clients have been changed to ensure privacy

FOREWORD

A client who got this book in pre-publication form wrote me an email saying she couldn't read it - some of the stories were too re-stimulating of her own traumas. She said, "I hope in the future I will be able read the book and not get upset. Guess I'm just too sensitive!!!!????!!!!"

I suggested that she tap (using EFT) while she was reading it, either repeatedly up and down all the points as she read, or tapping just on the karate chop point, whichever seemed to work best for her.

That turned out to be a good idea. She ended up reading the whole book, finding it very useful, and offering a list of grammar and spelling corrections! (Thank you!) As a result of her comments, we have placed the instructions about how to do EFT near the beginning of the book.

I recommend that you pay attention to your inner responses as you read, and take note of what specifically brings up an emotional reaction in you. Tap while you read: actually stop right then and tap for anything that particularly captures your attention and makes you feel sad or fearful. Or maybe you find yourself caught in a memory that re-stimulates feelings that you have been trying to keep buried.

If you take care of yourself while you explore this book, just the simple act of reading it can be a healing experience for you.

NOTES

Profoundly light-hearted strategies for unsticking stuck stuff

Self Portrait
by David Whyte

It doesn't interest me if there is one God
or many gods.
I want to know if you belong or feel
abandoned.
If you can know despair or see it in others.
I want to know
If you are prepared to live in the world
with its harsh need
to change you. If you can look back
with firm eyes
saying this is where I stand. I want to know
if you know
how to melt into that fierce heat of living
falling toward
the center of your longing. I want to know
if you are willing
to live, day by day, with the consequence of love
and the bitter
unwanted passion of your sure defeat.

I have heard, in *that* fierce embrace, even
the gods speak of God.

NOTES

Profoundly light-hearted strategies for unsticking stuck stuff

1
ARE YOU A HIGHLY *Sensitive* PERSON?

Have You Ever Heard:

Oh, you are just too sensitive!
You take things so hard!
Just let it roll off your back.
Why can't you just let it go!
And maybe even,
What's wrong with you?
You are such a cry baby!

**Maybe you thought
they were right - that there must be
something wrong with you!**

Being sensitive is not only a real emotional temperament, it is the kind of awareness that can save the world.

I speak as a "highly sensitive person" myself. It has taken me most of my life to understand this temperament and value it for its gifts. In my work as an Intuitive Mentor I have worked with many people like you or your loved ones.

If you're reading this and feeling, "Yeah, that's me, alright!" YOU are the help that is on the way, whether you are sensitive yourself, or partnered, working or interacting with, or the parent of someone who is sensitive.

Being sensitive is not only a real Emotional Temperament - it's the kind of awareness that can save the world

We Are Shaping the Future

I believe that in a real way the future depends on people like us. We are like the canary in the mine.

Do you remember the stories about the miners that took a canary in a cage down into the mine to find out if the air was safe to breathe down there? If the canary died, the miners didn't go down. The canary pointed the way for them; it ensured their safety.

I believe that highly sensitive people are pointing the way for all of humanity, toward learning a more graceful way of living. I believe that in some way we don't quite understand, the world has called each of us to be here, for our specific gifts.

Do These Statements Apply to You?

Make a copy of this list. Check the box on the left of each statement if it is at least somewhat true for you; leave the box unchecked if it is not very true or not at all true for you.

- ☐ I am easily overwhelmed by strong sensory input.
- ☐ I seem to be aware of subtleties in my environment.
- ☐ Other people's moods affect me.
- ☐ I tend to be very sensitive to pain.
- ☐ I find myself needing to withdraw during busy days: into a darkened room, or any place where I can have some privacy & relief from stimulation.
- ☐ I am particularly sensitive to the effects of caffeine.
- ☐ I am easily overwhelmed by things like bright lights, strong smells, coarse fabrics, or sirens close by.
- ☐ I have a rich, complex inner life.
- ☐ Loud noises make me very uncomfortable.

THIS IS WHERE I STAND

❑ I am deeply moved by the arts or music.

❑ My nervous system sometimes feels so frazzled that
   I just have to go off by myself.

❑ I am conscientious.

❑ I startle easily.

❑ I get rattled when I have a lot to do in a short
   amount of time.

❑ When people are uncomfortable in a physical
   environment I tend to know what needs to be done
   to make it more comfortable (like changing the
   lighting or the seating).

❑ I am annoyed when people try to get me to do
   too many things at once.

❑ I try hard to avoid making mistakes or forgetting
   things.

❑ I make a point to avoid violent movies and TV shows.

❑ I become unpleasantly aroused when a lot is going
   on around me.

❑ Being very hungry creates a strong reaction in
   me, disrupting my concentration or mood.

❑ Changes in my life shake me up.

❑ I notice and enjoy delicate or fine scents, tastes,
   sounds, works of art.

❑ I find it unpleasant to have a lot going on at once.

Profoundly light-hearted strategies for unsticking stuck stuff

THIS IS WHERE I STAND

☐ I make it a high priority to arrange my life to avoid upsetting or overwhelming situations.

☐ I am bothered by intense stimuli, like loud noises or chaotic scenes.

☐ When I must compete or be observed while performing a task, I become so nervous or shaky that I do much worse than I would otherwise.

☐ When I was a child, my parents or teachers seemed to see me as sensitive or shy.

NOTES

2
THE IDEALIST-HEALER TEMPERAMENT

Using the Meyers Briggs Model:

The Highly Sensitive Person is called the "Idealist Healer" (INFP)

Abstract in thought and speech
Cooperative
Introverted
Appear reserved and shy
Diplomatic
Empathic
Hunger for deep and meaningful relationships
Value personal growth, authenticity and integrity
Internally deeply caring
Deeply committed to the positive and the good
A mission to bring peace to the world
Strong personal morality
Often make extraordinary sacrifices for someone or something they believe in

Imagination and evolution are the goal

Seek unity, feel divided inside
Often had an unhappy childhood
May have been raised in a practical, industrious,
    social family
Didn't conform to parental expectations
Often feel isolated, "like an alien"
See themselves as ugly ducklings
Rich fantasy world as a child, may have been
    discouraged or punished for this by parents

Wish to please, try to hide their differences
Believe and are told that their sensitivity is bad

Drawn toward purity but continuously on the lookout
    for the wickedness they think lurks in them
Self-sacrificing to an extreme, in atonement for
    their failings
Keep this inner struggle hidden from others

Examples from history:
*Homer, Virgin Mary, Hans Christian Andersen,
Princess Diana, Gandhi, Shakespeare*

Resources:
Adapted from David Kiersey, *Please Understand Me II*
The Myers-Briggs Personality Type Indicator

Profoundly light-hearted strategies for unsticking stuck stuff

3

YOU MEAN THERE'S NOTHING WRONG WITH ME?

What Are the Traits of an HSP?

Elaine Aron
of HSPerson.com, introduced the idea of "the highly sensitive person."

She is a therapist who is highly sensitive herself, and in her practice she kept noticing that sensitive people seemed more susceptible to developing emotional challenges than people who were less acutely aware of their surroundings.

If you find you are a highly sensitive person, or your child is, then you need to be aware of the following points:

✳ *The trait of being sensitive* is normal--it is inherited by 15 to 20% of the population, and indeed the same percentage seems to be present in all higher animals.

✳ *Being an HSP means your* nervous system is more sensitive to subtleties. Your sight, hearing, and sense of smell are not necessarily keener (although they may be). But your brain processes information and reflects on it more deeply.

✳ *Being an HSP also means,* necessarily, that you are more easily overstimulated, stressed out, overwhelmed.

✳ *This trait is not something* new I discovered - it has been mislabeled as shyness (not an inherited trait), introversion (30% of HSPs are actually extraverts), inhibition, fearfulness, and the like.

HSPs can be these, but none of these are the fundamental trait they have inherited.

✳ *The reason for these* negative misnomers and general lack of research on the subject is that, in this culture, being tough and outgoing is the preferred or ideal personality - not high sensitivity (therefore, in the past the research focus has been on sensitivity's potential *negative impact* on sociability and boldness, not the *phenomenon* itself or its purpose).

✳ *This cultural bias* (see above) affects HSPs as much as their trait affects them, as I am sure you realize. Even those who loved you probably told you, "don't be so sensitive," making you feel abnormal when in fact you could do nothing about it, and you are not abnormal at all.

Kyra Mesich, Psy.D

KyraMesich.com, *author of* **The Sensitive Person's Survival Guide**, *has written widely about emotional sensitivity.*

Interestingly, the traits are a set of characteristics that have always had their own air of mystery. I'm referring to a set of psychological traits that has never been adequately explained before. These characteristics are commonly referred to as emotional sensitivity.

Profoundly light-hearted strategies for unsticking stuck stuff

Empathic people have observable traits that are easily identified

Sensitivity is a set of character traits that has just begun receiving attention from the psychological community within the past few years. This is strange, because it has always been fairly prevalent among the population.

Nevertheless, it has not even been officially recognized as a personality type. I want to make sure that you understand what I mean when I use the term sensitivity.

Attributes of emotionally sensitive people:

❋ *Emotionally sensitive people* feel emotions often and deeply. They feel as if they "wear their emotions on their sleeves."

❋ *They are keenly aware* of the emotions of people around them.

❋ *Sensitive people are easily* hurt or upset. An insult or unkind remark will affect them deeply.

❋ *In a similar vein, sensitive* people strive to avoid conflicts. They dread arguments and other types of confrontations because the negativity affects them so much.

✳ *Sensitive people are not* able to shake off emotions easily. Once they are saddened or upset by something, they cannot just switch gears and forget it.

✳ *Sensitive people are greatly* affected by emotions they witness. They feel deeply for others' suffering. Many sensitive people avoid sad movies or watching the news because they cannot bear the weighty emotions that would drive to their core and stick with them afterwards.

✳ *Sensitive people are prone* to suffer from recurrent depression, anxiety or other psychological disorders.

✳ *On the positive side,* sensitive people are also keenly aware of and affected by beauty in art, music and nature. They are the world's greatest artists and art appreciators.

✳ *Sensitive people are prone* to stimulus overload. That is, they can't stand large crowds, loud noise, or hectic environments. They feel overwhelmed and depleted by too much stimuli.

✳ *Sensitive people are born* that way. They were sensitive children.

Sensitive Kids
There are a couple different responses kids have to their own sensitivity.

One type of sensitive child is the stereotypical kid who gets picked on by bullies, and is, simultaneously, a well-behaved, good student because she cannot stand the thought of getting into trouble.

Profoundly light-hearted strategies for unsticking stuck stuff

The other type of sensitive child more often experiences the stimulus overload mentioned in the previous paragraph. Feeling over-stimulated, they have difficulty focusing, which causes them problems in school.

Sensitive people typically exhibit all or nearly all of the above descriptors:

One of the sure signs of a truly sensitive person is feeling animosity toward his own sensitive nature.

Many sensitive adults have learned to hide their sensitivity from others.

They feel like their sensitivity is a weakness.
They wish things didn't bother them so much.
They wish their emotions weren't so obvious to other people.
They wish they could let things go and not worry so much.
They aren't comfortable with their sensitivity, and wish they could do something to get rid of it (or at least get rid of the negative aspects of it).

Most sensitive people whole-heartedly wish they were tougher and more thick-skinned

NOTES

4
WHAT DO THE DOCTORS SAY?

What Does Modern Medicine Have to Say About Sensitivity?

Well, not much, it turns out!
And most of it is in the "it's all in your head, dear" category.

But there are a few enlightened physicians. Nancy Selfridge is one. She and I developed the *Freedom from Fibromyalgia* class together. Nancy is Chief of the Complementary Medicine and Wellness Center of Group Health HMO in Madison, Wisconisn.

Nancy cured herself from fibromyalgia by creating a protocol for it from the work of Dr. John Sarno, who believes that all pain and most chronic disease has at its source repressed emotion, especially anger.

Normal doctors don't know what to do with fibromyalgia patients

Nancy talks about sensitivity, fibromyalgia, pain, stress, and her own medical school training, which she identifies as the trigger for her illness (from ACEP conference 2005): *

Normal doctors don't know what to do with fibromyalgia patients. Some of it is the helplessness of medical science in this area. But some of it I believe is the exact temperament of the patient.

Fibromyalgia Patients

My fibromyalgia patients qualify as highly sensitive people. They've been identified as sensitive by other people in their environments. In my practice, every single one of them who has ever taken a Meyers-Briggs temperament inventory is an intuitive-feeler.

Except for two: one was evenly split intuitive-sensing-feeler, and the other one was evenly split thinking-feeling, but was intuitive. I think that's noteworthy. That's called 'the idealist temperament' by David Keirsey, Ph.D. who wrote *Please Understand Me II.*

Hyperbole and Metaphor

The language of the idealist is hyperbolic and metaphoric. You go into a physician and you're speaking in hyperbole: 'I can't stand the pain!! It is the worst pain I have ever had, and I can never get rid of it!!!' - and metaphor: 'There is a Tasmanian devil poking me with a hot poker in my hip!' To the typical, left-brained physician, you look weird. You can't do that in a doctor's office. If you can't say what's wrong with you in three sentences, you've lost that doctor.

Profoundly light-hearted strategies for unsticking stuck stuff

Communicate Your Symptoms

I'll even tell my patients, 'Listen, when you go to another doctor, like a specialist, you just write and rewrite until you can say what you need to say in three sentences. Because otherwise you're going to lose that doctor. They're going to think you're weird.' I know, I am one. I had to learn to talk the way they do.

Benevolence

The idealist is also invested in benevolence. So if we talk about people who are coming from idealism and spirituality, we're talking about their experience of the culture and the world that we're in, and multiple layers of potential emotional difficulty and struggling. We're talking about a sensory processing sensitivity. We are talking about a person who might get subjected to trauma just trying to live a normal life on planet Earth.

Temperament

So I believe that most of the people who get fibromyalgia have this substrate of temperament. And then they get sick. I think it reflects, and maybe we'll prove it one day with functional MRI studies, a brain that is more sensitive to stress and trauma, and more sensitive to getting into amplification mode after repeated stress and trauma.

We must **honor** the **sensitive temperament**

What's noteworthy about this is it may provide us with potential for intervention before things get carried away. One of the things Rue and I try to do in our work is help people understand that it is okay to honor the sensitive temperament in order to be well.

The literature says that people who are wired this way need periods of no and low stimulation in order to achieve homeostasis.

What does American culture look like? How many people are regularly meditating? How many people are willfully saying, 'I'll take less money to work part time?'

My own medical culture says: 'The work week is 60 hours, no less.' I work 40 hours a week and I'm considered part-time. I'm a part-time doctor. I choose not to be on call, so I'm considered a pariah.

Stress As Usual

We live in such a stressful culture. I think the World Health Organization said that one of the number one epidemics in the world right now is stress.

Some people are so stressed that they don't even recognize their stress, they think it is life as usual

Profoundly light-hearted strategies for unsticking stuck stuff

School can be quite traumatic as well. Kindergarten was okay for me, but first grade was horrible. I threw up at least 3 times a week almost for half a year and I kept going to school. That's insane.

We have these triggers, and they can be single event or cumulative stressors. I don't think it was a single event for me in my medical training, I think it was my sensitivity, plus just a lot piled on, including the fact that I discovered I am a person who should absolutely not work more than forty hours per week…oh, well…

This fits the neuro-plasticity model for pain generation that we've known about for ages. I studied this in med school. This just says that you can take an organism, let's say mammals, and you can subject that animal to a painful stimulus again and again, and the animal will begin responding with the pain response at lower and lower levels.

So you start with a shock at 10 and sooner or later you get to a level of one, and the organism is still startling and responding with the pain response.

A **sensitive** system is a nervous system that has **fewer filters** on it than is considered the norm

Now these people are rare people. This is a nervous system

that seems to have an element of vulnerability to stress and trauma anyway…maybe in the ways that the nervous system tends to be over activated in our particular cultural context.

People need to understand that if we're talking about a hard-wired way of processing information, *this is not psychopathology, and this is something that we would not necessarily want to change.*

These are the people who become the spiritual leaders and the medicine men and women and healers in our culture… you don't really want to change these things.

I've looked at people in my practice that I can identify as sensitive, but they haven't gotten sick. Why is that? Some of it is that they haven't had trauma triggering events. Some of them have, but they have adapted their lifestyles to meet their own needs.

I remember one guy in particular never had any symptoms in his whole life. He had a completely supportive family, very much a cocoon type of family who completely accepted his oddities. Even I thought he was a little bit odd. He got his master's degree in poetry.

Then he was supporting himself by being an editor of an online magazine. He worked entirely out of his house.

He wouldn't answer his phone. Just had the phone take messages. He kept his door locked, and didn't answer it when people came to the door. I thought…I want your life!

Profoundly light-hearted strategies for unsticking stuck stuff

He had complete control over the stimulation in his life. He achieved massive amounts of low and no stimulation.

A person who has a sensitive temperament and also has a belief system that grounds them in having to be a good boy or girl, is sort of set up for problems. They live a life as an "ultra" prototype. They act Very Good. Achieve. Follow the rules. Go the extra mile, often at their own expense. It's deadly. Inevitably, it creates a lot of symptoms.

* *From the transcript of Nancy Selfridge's presentation to the Association for Comprehensive Energy Psychology Conference, 2005.*

NOTES

Profoundly light-hearted strategies for unsticking stuck stuff

5
INTROVERT OR EXTROVERT?

Some sensitive people are introverts, and some are extroverts.

It all depends on your own personal source of renewal. How do you recharge your energy? What depletes your energy?

Rue:
No More Birthdays!

I am a highly sensitive introvert. When I was four, or so the family story goes, my mother organized a big birthday party for me at my house. After the party, I told her, "NEXT year I am going to stay in my room the whole time!"

For some sensitive kids,
Parties = Torture

In the old photo of the party, you can see all the little kids and their moms with big grins, sitting there in happy rows in my family's living room. And there I am in the first row, my four-year-old face looking grumpy, tortured and stony.

I need lots of time by myself. I love the deep connecting work that I do with people - that nourishes me. And I love teaching classes and talking to groups, even large ones, if it is a subject that I know about and am passionate about.

But I hate parties, or groups of people where I don't know anyone, or any activity that will require me to do the surface "chit chat." My husband has given up on taking me to his work functions.

I used to think I was anti-social

If I am not doing a vitalizing activity, being in groups of people drains me. I used to think I was anti-social, and maybe I am! I just know that if it's my priority to keep myself Well and Rested - and it is - groups of people are not for me.

From Sophia:
A Sensitive Introvert

I was isolated and very quiet. I kept to myself. I can't handle very much stimulation at one time. I pick up way too much of other peoples' stuff.

In Alanon I found being in the group so overwhelming. I find I can zero into other people's pain, their issues. I learned there that most people aren't as sensitive as I am.

I can't deal with it. I get overwhelmed, even though I know this sensitivity is a gift. So I tend to avoid other people.

I have gotten so good at avoiding everything

As soon as I get over-stimulated, it makes more pain, so I avoid it. I have gotten so good at avoiding everything. I'm a combination of sensitivity and toughness. I've toughed it through a lot of stuff. As a child I learned how not to show what I was feeling. My mom didn't like sensitivity in her children. We learned really quickly not to show or say our feelings. I was really quiet, didn't get involved with other people.

I'm a combination of sensitivity and toughness

In my years married to a drinker I would go to the bar with him, but I would drink tomato juice. I never participated, I sat with my back against the wall. I looked after everybody. Afterwards I would lie awake from all that I had experienced. I was devastated by all the pain that all these people were in. I didn't understand that I had a more than average ability to feel other people's stuff.

I didn't understand that I had a more than average ability to feel other peoples' stuff

From Sandra:
A Sensitive Extrovert

I actually feel like I lived most of my life over here to the side of my body. I didn't want anyone to see me, it was too dangerous. So I created a lot of clamorous, extroverted activity so no one would see me.

I actually feel like
I lived most of my life over here
to the side of my body

To others, I seemed very extroverted. I also drank socially. It took the cork out of my inhibitions. I would be very amusing, a great storyteller. Creating a whirlwind, activity, noise, interesting things to look at or hear, so no one would ever notice the real me over there. A diversionary camoflage.

Creating a whirlwind, activity, noise,
interesting things to look at or hear,
so no one would ever notice
the real me over there

It is not that it was inauthentic. It is what I would do if I could really be alive. Life really comes down to knowing, "do I like this or not?" When you are outside your body you don't know. There is this terrible starvation going on. I am terrified of intimacy. *You* are not there.

I lost the ability to be alone with my self, or to be myself or with anyone else.

There is this terrible starvation going on

Unbeknownst to me, I was deeply unhappy, but I thought that was just the deal. I think that my mother was to some extent - maybe deeply - unhappy, and *she* thought that was just the deal.

It isn't necessary to be that unhappy. We couldn't have understood that. I think she thinks that a life is basically unhappy but you just do it anyway.

There is the soldiering on. My dad just didn't go to the emotions. Neither mom nor dad was available to me emotionally.

I was deeply unhappy,
but I thought that was just the deal

Now, if I am alone long enough to be still inside I am getting to the point where I can tell how I feel. I need a lot of solitude to settle into my body, feel alive.

I can stay with myself now and tell how I'm feeling. I walk my dog at night near the lake. At night it is so beautiful. I noticed that once the people are all gone, the atmosphere changes. Everything is very still and very present. At first when I did this I would cry. I would walk and cry every night. Gradually I would feel joy. Peace.

Now I notice when something feels a certain kind of beautiful, true, authentic, spiritual. There is a touchstone inside me. Now I know how to feel positive. Now, it is quite interesting to be with people when I choose to, when I feel like it. This is all new for me.

There is a touchstone inside me
Now I know how to feel positive
This is all new for me

Profoundly light-hearted strategies for unsticking stuck stuff

6
THE WORLD IS MY ORACLE

The world has something to say through us, and to us

On the five hour drive back to my home in Wisconsin from visiting my mother in Illinois recently, I was pondering how to write this book about sensitivity. I wanted a theme that I could weave throughout the narrative that held it altogether. Nothing was coming to me. So I did this trick that I often do when I am in need of answers or insights.

I ask the world to be my oracle

I say, "OK, World, I'm wondering about this question here. I need your help. I am going to pay close attention to what comes into my awareness in the next 20 minutes. I trust that you will send me some wisdom."

In this case, I added, "And even though there isn't much going on here in the corn fields and the highway, you, universe, are infinitely creative, and that won't be a problem for you.

So I promise to pay extra close attention so that I don't miss your response."

Then I just pay attention.

The wonderful thing about using the world as my oracle is that I become acutely aware of my presence in it, and my relationship to everything.

Everything comes alive!

Everything has the potential of being a source of wisdom for me. Everything feels extraordinarily friendly, as if it is reaching out to me. I find myself in connection with the world in a vital, vibrant way that I am more often than not asleep to.

Clues

Right away after I made my pronouncement, I drove under an overpass. It had the name of the road written on it: "Welland."

Hmmmm, I thought, wondering how it applied, as I drove on.

The next thing that caught my attention, after a long stretch of semi trucks without anything interesting on their trailers, was a big billboard that had the curious, irritating, but largely irrelevant words: "The Heart Breakers. Join the Gentleman's Club." OK, we can give that one a miss…

After awhile, I realized that I really had to go to the bathroom. I was traveling with my not-quite-year-old dog who was sleeping through the trip for the first time and so I had kept driving, trying to maximize this opportunity for quiet drive time. But I had really gone past my limit some time ago. So when a rest area came up, we exited and did our business.

Time's Up!

Getting back on the road, I checked the time and thought, "Oh, rats! My 20 minutes is up! Not much to show for it…"

…Well, there was "Welland. "
And "rest area."
Hmmmm, what could I do with that?

Ummm… Well and Rested? And what would be the opposite of well and rested? Why, Sick and Tired, of course!

Sick and Tired!

✳ How often do we say to ourselves, "I am just sick and tired of _____ !"?

✳ How many of us are sick and tired of being so darned sensitive?

✳ Of falling yet again into despondency over someone's unthinking comment?

✳ About feeling left out?

✳ Sick and tired of feeling overwhelmed?

✳ Sick and tired of feeling like we don't measure up – again? Sick and tired of being so emotional?

✳ Of being teased?

✳ Of toughing it out all by ourselves?

✳ Sick and tired of feeling like we are the only one who cares?

How many of us are in fact LITERALLY
sick and tired?
In pain?
Depressed?
Sad?
Fearful?
Angry?

Let's explore together how to
Create Sensitivity Magic
where Sensitivity Misery has
been living!

Transform *Sick and Tired* into *Well and Rested!*

As the canaries in the mine, we have learned a lot about how to live and think in a way that makes people sick and tired. And that makes the world sick and tired.

The more we can learn about transforming that way of living a life, the better we can model what generates wellness and restfulness, peace and calm.

The world
needs
what we know!

Profoundly light-hearted strategies for unsticking stuck stuff

NOTES

Profoundly light-hearted strategies for unsticking stuck stuff

7
BE
SELF-ISH!

The Idealists

Who comes first?
Deep down inside we are such good people. We are so committed to bringing goodness into the world.

But actually for many of us, this is exactly what leads us to being so sick and so tired.

More often than not we put our commitment to "saving the world" ahead of our own well-being. In fact, many of us have the unconscious belief that we must "save the world" before we can attend to our own needs.

Remember our wonderful ideal qualities:

* *Internally deeply caring*
* *Deeply committed to the positive and the good*
* *On a mission to bring peace to the world*
* *Strong personal morality*
* *Often make extraordinary sacrifices for someone/ something we believe in*

Interestingly, sensitive people often fail to include themselves in this mission. The other day when I pointed out to my client how good she is to OTHER people, she said to me in surprise,

"Of course I would never let anyone else down! But it hadn't occurred to me that I let MYSELF down."

Sometimes we intentionally leave ourselves off the list, in an attempt not to be "selfish."

Self-ish?

When someone mentions being selfish to me, I always reframe it. I say, "How about spelling "selfish" with a capital S – make it "Selfish." I draw a big S in the air. The capital S stands for your soul.

If you don't take care of your soul, no one else will

So go on and BE SELF-ISH!! You have the right. You deserve that!

Another client, primed by me to think of herself as having a highly sensitive temperament, took the temperament test offered in the book *Please Understand Me II* by David Kiersey.

She is the kind of person who is Very Focused on Doing Things Right (aren't we?!!), so when she took the test she second-guessed all the questions and answered them the way she thought she should be!

When she scored the test and it looked like she wasn't an idealist after all, she broke down and cried. I encouraged her to go back and take the test again, and this time, notice what the first response from her heart was.

We have lots of ways of taking ourselves off of our "to do" list, and so often people are surprised to discover that they aren't even on their own list. Putting oneself at the TOP of your own "to do" list is a revolutionary idea.

NOTES

Profoundly light-hearted strategies for unsticking stuck stuff

8
THE POWER OF BELIEF!

How did we get to such a sorry *sick and tired* state of affairs??

Our family's belief system about self worth and what is possible for us in the world has deep impact on our lives.

We literally pick up our family's belief system at the cellular level on our way into incarnation. We grew up in the midst of these beliefs, not even noticing that they might be REALLY skewed. We were just like fish taking the water they swim in for granted.

When you were younger
Did you go visit your friends' families and wonder (or envy, or be alarmed) about how they did things so differently from your family?

You believed your family was "normal!" There is a culture to a family, a "way it's s'posed to be," and there are clear rewards and punishments for straying from these expectations.

Profoundly light-hearted strategies for unsticking stuck stuff

Our beliefs about who we are and what is possible in the world arise from our families.

Our survival depends on conforming to what our parents expect of us. That is the raw stuff we come into the world to learn how to integrate - or transform.

Examples

As you read the following, think about what YOUR family believes (unspoken messages are in parentheses).

Some Misaligned Family Beliefs:

BE PERFECT

* Death is better than making the wrong decision
* We don't talk about unpleasant things
* Don't get mad, get even
* What will people think?

TRY HARDER

* (What you are doing is not good enough)

PLEASE ME, TAKE CARE OF ME

* (Your needs are less important than mine)

HURRY UP
✳ (What you are doing is not important)

BE STRONG
✳ Big boys don't cry

✳ Tough it out, soldier on, you can take it, you just have to get through this

What is a poor highly sensitive idealist person, feeling alien, misplaced, and out of place in an abrasive culture to do?

Well, fortunately, we are angels in disguise, and so we have RESOURCES!

Resources right here!
One of our best resources is quite literally at our very fingertips.

Emotional Freedom Techniques (tapping) is one of many new tools that can help us to uncover what keep us from putting ourselves on our own personal and planetary To Do list (see chapters 18 & 19 for extensive, illustrated information on how to use EFT for your own limiting beliefs).

I have worked with many people who present themselves as Sick and Tired, but who are really HSP/Idealists looking for a way to be Well and Rested. A Well and Rested person radiates healing energy.

A Well and Rested person is an actual force for healing in the world, simply by being here

There are no expectations to meet. There are no requirements.
You don't have to Know Everything first. You don't have to
Figure it Out. You have your own internal sensing system
that lets you know What is Right for You. It all comes down
to knowing this: is it Yum or Yuck?

Here are some stories about some Sensitive/Idealist people
who are discovering their own internal Yum and Yuck
Yardstick, tapping their way to getting Well and Rested.

Profoundly light-hearted strategies for unsticking stuck stuff

9
WE ARE BORN GOOD!

Feeling worthless

What ever happens to us as children that is less than we deserve seems to end up in a simmering pot of beliefs about not being good enough. The labels on the pot read "helpless, hopeless, worthless." A sense of "unworthiness" seems to be endemic among humans, at least in the West.

I believe that the devilish problem of starving for self worth that haunts us at every step in our lives is, in fact, an angel/ally/teacher in disguise.

We can't take a pill to make that feeling go away, or have surgery to cut it out. Might the emotional pain of low self-esteem hold our feet to the fire? Are we being asked to enlarge our sense of who and why we are, in order to hold how we see ourselves differently?

Our whole lives are about being shaped by living the questions that arise from our struggle toward knowing that we are "enough." This issue of feeling like we need to "measure up" is like the grain of sand in the oyster shell of human consciousness. It keeps coming up, and we keep returning to it, mulling it over, working it, deeper and deeper, so that eventually we will get to some truth about it.

As highly sensitive idealists we value personal growth, and when it is awakened in us we have a natural capacity to seek a deeper meaning in what we encounter. We already have a yearning toward a vision of a better world - we feel it in our very cells. We know things could/should/will be better, and we are willing to make extraordinary sacrifices to manifest something we believe in.

I believe that each of us is doing this on behalf of all of us. The insights and transformations and healing that each of us accomplishes helps to clear the way for the larger being of humanity.

Spiritual teacher David Spangler (lorian.org) has this interesting reframe for "unworthiness:"

Let us contrast unworthiness with incompleteness or insufficiency. I have a one cup measuring pitcher and a two-cup measuring pitcher.

If I need to measure out two cups of water, I would not say to the one cup measure "you are unworthy of receiving this water because you are not a two-cup measure."

Instead, I would say, "you are insufficient to what is needed,

Profoundly light-hearted strategies for unsticking stuck stuff

but you are perfect for receiving a cup of water." If I don't have a two-cup measure, then using the one-cup measure twice will give me the sufficiency I need.

Often in life we may find ourselves in a condition in which we are insufficient to receive what could be received or fulfill what must be fullfilled. This does *not* mean we are unworthy, only that we are *in the moment* incomplete, relative to the task, and insufficient relative to the need.

Growth is indicated. Or there may be ways I can turn my insufficiency into sufficiency by re-imagining and rethinking how to fulfill the need and also who I am, like accepting the one-cup identity of my measuring cup and using it twice, not wasting time bemoaning that I don't have a two-cup measure instead.

Unworthiness implies a flawed condition, even one that is static and irreparable. There is nothing flawed about a one-cup measuring cup. For certain recipes it is ideal, and even at times overly sufficient, as when a recipe calls for a half-cup of something. Nothing has to be repaired or redeemed about a one-cup measure. It is only that. for certain tasks, it is insufficient. or the task needs to be redefined and re-imagined so that its apparent limitation becomes an asset rather than a liability, like using it twice (or as many times as needed) to measure out the right amount of liquid.

Unworthiness stops us and says we cannot go further, but insufficiency only forces us to re-strategize so that we can continue in new, and perhaps unexpected, ways.

So, if I say I, as a personality, as a person, as an incarnate

Profoundly light-hearted strategies for unsticking stuck stuff

being, am unworthy, I may be drawing a boundary about myself that truly limits me and stops the flow of my growth.

If I acknowledge that I may be insufficient, and that this is not a judgment or a flaw, but only a recognition of the extent of my capacity at any given moment, then I can still move forward through a process of re-imagination.

I think the feeling of unworthiness can be bottomless. How much must I accomplish or do or be before I feel worthy? There will always be dimensions, energies, presences, tasks, and so forth to which I do not measure up, for which I am not ready or sufficient. Must I always feel unworthy, then?

Let me see what I am sufficient for. Let me not try to overcome unworthiness but rather find that for which I am sufficient and worthy and begin there.

Am I worthy to be loved? No, some part of me says.

Does that mean no part of me is worthy to be loved? Is my toe unworthy of love? Is my finger? *What specific part of me is unworthy of love or sacredness or spirit?* Can I locate that part? Is there a part of me that I CAN love or imagine God as loving? Maybe it's just a hair on my head. Maybe it's a fingernail. Maybe it's one cell in the lining of my stomach.

Unworthiness seems to me to be "preemptive fear." It's like novice public speakers who feel constrained to apologize in advance for any deficiencies in the presentation they are about to make, letting the audience know that they know it will not be perfect. This apologia is often a strategy to deflect criticism which they feel will - indeed, must - come.

A feeling of unworthiness can be a mask for fear of being rebuffed or criticized, of being vulnerable and open and then being smacked down or rejected. It is preemptive rejection.

It can be an excuse not to take a stand, a mask for inertia. Rather than take a risk, we can hang back in our lives and say, "Well, I can't do that or accept that because, you see, I'm too unworthy."

Of course, unworthiness is an expression of ego in its stuck and limiting state. It's a way of identifying ourselves. Better to be unworthy than not to exist at all. I whine, therefore I am!

Not willing to risk feeling worthy ourselves - for who knows what accountabilities, tasks, responsibilities, honors, energy, challenges, and engagements may come our way if we proclaim ourselves worthy - we don't want anyone else to feel worthy, either. So we withhold statements of worth and honor, love and appreciation from each other. We enter into a conspiracy of mediocrity and fear by spreading the idea that we are all unworthy.

And if someone dares to rise above us by saying, "I am worthy, Lord. I can take all the light and love and splendor you can bestow one me, and I can take all the tasks that you may deem me fit to meet!" then we must tear that person down. For they challenge us. They challenge the lies we tell about ourselves and each other. They challenge our fears and our shadows.

We are complicit in a conspiracy of unworthiness.

Profoundly light-hearted strategies for unsticking stuck stuff

Who is easier to control, to lead, to manipulate, to bind and oppress, the person who proclaims himself or herself worthy and powerful, or the one who hides herself or himself in sackcloth and ashes?

Who might feel safest, the one who cowers in preemptive self-rejection, or the one who stands up and says, "Here I am! Let me engage the world, with all it contains of sorrow and joy, darkness and light, for there is that in me that which can bless and heal, liberate and empower. There is that in me that is an ally for all that would grow and prosper and reveal the love that is the ground of all our beings!"?

If we would change this, do we not need to tell ourselves a different story about ourselves? Do we not need to take up our courage and stand up, stand forth, and be loving, to ourselves as much as to anyone else? Do we not need to see and honor each other and tell a new narrative of who we are and why we are here?

In the beginning, we each and we all so loved this world, that we came to this place, to this moment in history, to be with each other, to stand here in love as allies and colleagues to bless this world as only we can do.

What comes next in the story is something only we can each add in our unique and powerful ways....

*(from online class, **Self Worth and the Inner Light**, 2002)*

Healing our sense of self worth is all about changing the story we tell ourselves about who we are and what we deserve. Here is a story by therapist and EFT practitioner

Deborah Mitnick, about her client who had felt guilty and worthless virtually all of his life. By the end of the session he understood who he was from a completely different perspective. He says: I realize now that God forgave me a long time ago, but I never forgave myself. Now I can forgive myself."

And He Cried On My Shoulder
By Deborah Mitnick, LCSW, trauma-tir.com

The following is a report of a recent session that I had with a new client. Details have been altered to preserve client confidentiality. The trauma was even more dramatic than the way I'm portraying it here.

The client is a 55-year-old who was referred to me by two psychiatrists. Forty-five years ago, "Henry" witnessed the death of a child-friend of his. His friend was disemboweled in front of his eyes during a school outing at a nature park. Henry has always felt responsible for the accident because he had encouraged his friend to attend the event where the accident took place.

Since that time, Henry has been unable to cry. He has felt guilty all of his life. He has never held a meaningful job. He has multiple allergies to food and to the environment.

He suffers from fungal infections, has debilitating physical pains, and many immune system problems. He suffers from bowel problems and daily headaches. He complains of low energy and dissatisfaction with life.

His strongest emotions are shame, guilt, and anger. He rates them all at a Subjective Unit of Distress Scale (SUDS) level of 9, with 10 being the worst it could be. He says that a 10 would mean that he couldn't cope any more.

He avoids making meaningful relationships and has distanced himself from most of his family and friends. He's left most of his jobs "in shame."

Henry has been in multiple therapies over the years, starting immediately after the accident. There have been at least six inpatient hospitalizations, at least 13 bilateral treatments with ECT (shock treatments), and multiple medications for depression, anxiety, and mania.

When Henry called me, he told me that he was afraid to remember the event and that he was afraid that he would get overwhelmed during the session and would "go crazy" again. He knew about me for four months before he actually scheduled the appointment. He's been "afraid to face what needs to be faced."

I met with the client for a "free consultation" for one hour. I told him that my job in the session was to keep him on task. I described my role as that of the secretary for the busy executive. I would keep him organized.

I told him that I had some tools that I could use that would provide him with the opportunity to do his own healing. I made it very clear to him that although I could not "cure" him, I would provide the structure and the environment to make it possible for him to find his own positive result. I also reminded him that in my work, there are no guarantees of success and I make no promises of a positive result, although my success-rate is very high.

After this first hour, we agreed to work together. I demonstrated the EFT tapping points and asked if he'd want to do his own tapping, or if he'd want me to tap for him. I received his consent to do the tapping for him.

I then conducted a formal and complete psychiatric interview. This helped me assess if the client had the ego-strengths to work through the trauma with the methods that I have to offer him.

When Henry mentioned his allergies, his low self-esteem, his difficulties with maintaining meaningful employment, I told him that some of the methods we would be using could be helpful to him in overcoming some of these problems.

Henry said, "This accident is something I've never been allowed to talk about. My father wouldn't let me talk about it at home, so I had to deal with it in my room alone. The sounds and smells haunt me. I've had no one to tell about it. My life has been hell since it happened. I guess I should bite the bullet and talk to you about it, but it's really too painful for me to address. I'm afraid if I start to tell you about it that I will go crazy and get too overwhelmed to continue. I'm afraid I'll run from your office, screaming and crying, and I'll never get over this problem."

I decided that we needed to "tap around" the trauma for a while. I asked him what physical symptoms he has that he associates with the trauma.

His throat always aches and feels tight. He feels like crying, but never does. We tapped for "this throat emotion" for a SUDS reduction from 8 to 5 1/2. At that point, he said that it's hard for him to express emotions about this, but his throat no longer ached or felt tight, yet he was afraid to let go of the tightness. So we tapped for "afraid to get over this tightness emotion."

New aspects began to emerge. He said, "I'm not sure what I saw. I feel responsible for what happened. I had nagged my friend to go on the outing with me."

(Please note: I still have no idea what the details are about this incident. You know as much as I do from this description.)

I decided to start providing him with "re-framing" possibilities. I asked him if he would have free will if someone encouraged him to go on an outing. Would he be "locked into" going, just because someone strongly encouraged him, or nagged him?

He looked thoughtful, and said, it would still be his choice.

I asked him to remember what he was like at age 10. Would he have been able to say "no" if someone encouraged him to do something and he didn't want to do it?

He agreed that he would have been able to say "no" to a friend, even at the age of 10.

We tapped for "this responsibility" and "this guilt."

His throat began to feel better. We tapped for "this beating myself up-thing." He reported feeling much more relaxed and "light." He said, "My throat is feeling a lot better. I'm no longer afraid that I won't be able to swallow."

To continue with the re-frames, I asked, "How old were you at the time of the incident?" He said he was only 10 years old. I said, "How much power does a 10 year old have over another person?" He smiled.

We returned to tapping on "this responsibility" and "this guilt." But this time, my suggested affirmations had to do with, "I was just a kid - doing the best I could at the time. I'm not responsible for the decisions of others," etc. Every time I do such an affirmation, I ask the person, "Does this ring true for you? I don't want to put words in your mouth that don't fit for you." Henry said that all that I had suggested was true for him.

He began to smile (first time in the session). He said, "This feels so much better. It's affirming to think of it that way. It's getting less intense in my throat. [He laughed.] It's now moved up to the roof of my mouth. I can feel it moving up and out!" He rated his throat constriction as a "1" now.

Henry grabbed my hand. He said, "I'll never forget this moment." He put his head on my shoulder and wept for about five minutes. (Remember, he hasn't cried for 45 years.) I just held him.

He doesn't know it, but I cried, too. I felt humbled by the power of the method. I felt thrilled for him that he had trusted himself, and trusted enough in me, to permit the healing to take place.

I thought about how simple healing could be, as well as how rapidly it could happen, but at the same time, it can be a profound experience. I also realized that it was not necessary for him to "barrel in" and feel the full pain of the incident. It was also not necessary for me to "understand" exactly what his trauma was.

He opened his eyes, sighed deeply, smiled at me, and closed his eyes. He stayed immobile for over five minutes. He finally said, "I'm forgiving myself. I thank God for bringing me to you. I thank God for revealing this method to me. I realize now that God forgave me a long time ago, but I never forgave myself. Now I can forgive myself."

Henry began to rub the center of his chest. He said, "I'm rubbing in the good feeling. I want to treasure this moment. Thank you for giving me the opportunity to find my voice and say what needed to be said. The balancing you did with the tapping made this possible."

This seemed like the perfect "end-point" of the session, and we stopped.

I still have no idea what happened during the trauma. You know everything that I know. Henry never reviewed the incident. We only "talked around" it. And it resolved.

I spoke to Henry two days after this session. Here's what he said: "I felt so good on Thursday. I'm so happy that I did that session with you. I've put the accident behind me. I don't have any guilt about that any more. I feel totally relieved about that accident. Now it's behind me. I don't think about it anymore. I really thank you for that."

This session lasted for 70 minutes.

What do you want?

The Women and Spirituality group that I facilitated was exploring the interesting question, "What is the difference between unconditional love and having no boundaries?"

One of the women was talking intensely and tearfully about the constant fights she and her partner seem to fall into, and how hard it is for her to stand up for herself. After she had lamented for awhile about the many different behaviors she didn't want to be stuck in anymore, I finally asked, "What do you want?"

It was as if she hadn't heard the question. She repeated again that she didn't want to have to do this, or go there, or be so accommodating all the time.

I had to ask her two more times before she finally said, "Oh. I guess I'm talking in negatives. You mean you want to know what I want? Oh God!"

That was hard to talk about, because there were lots of reasons why she thought she couldn't/shouldn't say what she wants, mostly having to do with believing that she does not deserve to have what she wants, and somehow believing that having what she wants probably wouldn't be a good thing anyway.

We took a few minutes to explore what it would mean for her to be able to say what she wants. That didn't come easily either. It was clear that she had for so long focused on what she didn't want that she hadn't considered what it would be like to actually ask for what she wanted. Or even to know what she wanted.

Profoundly light-hearted strategies for unsticking stuck stuff

My Family's Beliefs

It seemed like a good time to ask her about the family she grew up in. What was the belief culture of her birth family? What expectations had she come in with, or picked up along the way, that were influencing her current self-less behavior?

Life in Eileen's birth family was chaotic. It was a traditionally male dominated family with an emotionally weak man at the helm and an angry unpredictable wife.

"You had to tippy-toe around Dad. It was all about trying to please the man. I was the oldest of four children at five years old - I had to try not to fuss, and try to keep my three wild brothers out of trouble. I had to be the good one. I had to keep the peace and be good so that my mother didn't freak out. I could never ask for anything."

I had to be the Good One

I asked Eileen to think back to her childhood. What beliefs did you form about yourself as a result of having to be the good one and never ask for anything for yourself but never getting any praise either?

She thought a moment and then said:
I am not good enough.
What is wrong with me?

Pain, the Driver, the Teacher

I talked about the idea of seeing pain as a teacher. How the physical pain she had been suffering from over the last

Profoundly light-hearted strategies for unsticking stuck stuff

several years had driven her to begin to learn how to be good to herself. Then I asked her if there had been any specific injunctions in her family belief culture against being good to yourself.

"Oh yeah," she grinned. "My dad - when I came home with my report card full of A's... "

"Oh," I interrupted, "You mean he said, 'What happened with this one B here?'"

"No, no, he said 'Don't get the big head. Who do you think you are?'"

Who do you think you are?

We talked about what a powerful setup that was - it's a setup that makes it impossible to believe in yourself, or take recognition for any good that you had done.

"Ohhhh!" Eileen looked thoughtful. "I guess I think that I have to be so perfect all the time because if my goodness isn't earned, I can't take credit for it."

"But you can't ever earn your goodness!" I exclaimed. "You can't ever be perfect enough. Because with this set up you can never take credit for what you do....

"And therefore.... you can never be good to yourself," I said.

Pausing, I said it again, with a different emphasis: "You CAN...never be good to yourself." A different take on the same words, a prompt to her unconscious mind to see that how she treated herself was a choice, not an order. (The implication is that you can choose to "not ever be good to yourself," but there are other possiblities...)

You can - or can not - be good to yourself

I continued, "You have taken all this pain of your past, and your powerful deep anger which you can't express, and it has all gone into your body. The energy of all this emotion has nowhere to go!

"The pain of not being able to be perfect enough has gone into your body. The pain of not being able to express the goodness of who YOU really are has gone into your body. And you can't get well because if you do you would stand up for yourself, and then you might lose your relationship.

"So, Eileen. What is your choice? Will you stay ill in order to save your relationship?"

So then I asked Eileen to imagine that what ranged in front of her were all the parts of her that thought it wouldn't be such a good idea to stand up for herself in this way. To think of them as "bodies of information," so to speak.

And, even though they were showing up like inner goons and obstructions, to imagine that behind their appearance they had a positive intention. There was something positive they were trying to do for her but didn't know any other way to get it. What could that be?

This was an unfamiliar thought. She took it in slowly.

Profoundly light-hearted strategies for unsticking stuck stuff

"They're trying to keep me safe. But they want me to know that I will never be safe. I WILL NEVER BE SAFE. The only way to be safe is to go along, don't make waves. I learned that right away as a child growing up in the constant abuse and manipulation of my family."

"So," I said, "When you think about it, it is clear that there are lots and lots of people, millions of people, in the world who have that same belief. You can almost imagine it as a "beingness," also a body of information, a sort of magnetic trap that people can be entranced by. And maybe all of us have at least a little connection to it in some way. But some people live within it." As I talked I traced a shape in the air in front of her, as if it was right there.

What would it be like if you imagined that you could STEP OUT OF IT NOW, and step back, and observe this phenomenon that happens to humans, objectively, without judgment, just watching it?

She stared at the floor, taking several deep shuddery breaths, and at last said in a quiet voice, full of wonder, "I can see that it is just a belief. It is not The Truth (making her hands form the shape of a T). I thought it was The Truth. It is just a belief.

"Oh! Now I'm flashing on Israel and Palestine! That's exactly what is going on there! Both of those countries are gripped in the same belief that there is no other way to be or think than this one!"

I pretended to take hold of this shape in front of her, and move it way over to the side so it wouldn't still be in her face.

Profoundly light-hearted strategies for unsticking stuck stuff

And asked her, what is it like now, to move through your life knowing that you can step out of the enchantment of that belief any time?

Then she said something huge and wonderful. She said, slowly, "I understand that any time I abandon or dishonor myself, it is abuse. I want to learn to take care of myself. I want to be as good a friend to myself as I am to other people."

She is a gardener, so I invited her to imagine that she herself was a garden, being lovingly tended by a wise compassionate gardener. And then to imagine that she is the gardener - how do you take good care of a garden? You know how! ("Yeah - even weeds are just plants in the wrong place. In fact, I just let the weeds grow. A lot of them are healing herbs, or edible!")

We ended with a discussion and then a meditation on how as humans, our inner landscape is "peopled" with all these dark and bright magnetically enchanting shapes. And how (bringing in a thread from an earlier conversation) maybe healing doesn't mean "living happily ever after," but rather gaining and practicing the ability to step out of the influence of shapes that don't feel good to us, and choosing the shapes that feel right...

...and how these patterns of information are larger than ourselves, larger even than our human evolution. And that each time - each time! - any of us is able to step out of a limiting belief and consider it with a neutral yet compassionate eye, we do a great service for the evolution of consciousness.

One more story about goodness:

The only way we can know that we are good is to have that mirrored back to us by someone who believes it about us. Most of us grew up around people who hadn't had that mirror in their lives, so they didn't know how to hold it up for us so we could see the goodness in ourselves.

"Loreen" began our phone session by saying she was feeling emotionally exhausted. She has been learning how to change her story. This process has been a huge revelation for her, lots of three steps forward and two steps backward.

She has just recently touched into the little girl part of herself, the little Loreen who had been frantically running around looking for love in all the wrong places all of her life, and who was feeling the deep pain that in the adult Loreen has been diagnosed as fibromyalgia.

Loreen said, "I can't figure out how my parents couldn't have just loved me. Is there enough love to make up for what we didn't get?"

What a lovely, poignant question.

I said that her question came out of the assumption that if there is a finite amount of love given to us, we only have a finite amount of love to give in our lives. Is that what she believed?

"Well, no," she said. "I believe that I have an infinite amount of love to give."

We agreed that the more love you get the more you have to give, AND the more love you give the more you have to give.

So, I asked her, "Where in your body do you feel the love you have to give?"

"Wow! I hadn't thought about that!" she said. "It is around my heart, and it feels like holding something, like my arms are around something."

I asked her some questions to help her identify the exact physiological sensations even better. The more consciously you can feel a sensation in your body, the more real it becomes for you.

* Is it warmer or cooler?
* Is it moving or still?
* Is it silent or is there sound?
* Is it lighter or darker?
* Is it lighter or heavier?

Loreen said the love in her heart felt warmer, silent, more light, and lighter in density as well, and was radiant from her center in her chest. She loved the feeling in her. "I can feel a glow all through me," she said.

I noted that what she felt was the difference between feeling loved and being love. I suggested that she imagine that she could teach "Little Loreen" how to feel this way inside.

"Think about your parents," I said. "You thought they didn't love you. They seemed to treat you as if they didn't love you. But consider that they treated you the way they were treated.

They didn't know any better. And that means no one in your ancestry really knew how to do what you are learning to do now.

"Think of this: it means that how they treated you was not about you.   How they treated you was not about your value in the world. How they treated you was not about how much they loved you. How your parents treated you was all about how they learned to think of themselves from their own childhood. It was the manifestation of their own pain. That inheritance goes way back in your ancestry.

The important thing is this:
you are the first in your family history
who has the capacity to actually break the
bonds of that old family legacy.

"That makes me sad," Loreen said.

"So imagine this," I suggested. "Be strongly aware of this warm radiant feeling of being a source of infinite love that you have just now become aware of. See in your mind's eye your mother as she looked when you were a little girl.

If you can (emphasizing the words makes it a directive to her unconscious mind) imagine that a part of you can float over to be inside your mother, looking out of her eyes and feeling her feelings. Through her eyes, see little Loreen.

"Now, without any reference to your thoughts, emotions or memories of your mother, imagine that you can just fill your

Profoundly light-hearted strategies for unsticking stuck stuff

mother up with this inner warm, light radiant sense of love that you are experiencing now."

I paused to let Loreen explore this.

I continued, "Now, imagine that you can radiate this warm loving feeling from your mother to little Loreen as a flow of thoughts, energy, behaviors, feelings. Imagine that little Loreen can feel this sensation flowing to her from her mother, and that somehow it awakens this capacity to "be loved" in her as well."

After that I asked Loreen to float out of her mother's body, and be in her young self, feeling that love flowing to her from her mother.

Loreen took some moments to do all this. "I can feel my little Loreen feeling so good, warm, radiant, happy," she said. "It's an intense feeing, and I am seeing a lot of a beautiful red."

"So," I continued, "Drift off over to the side so you can see both little Loreen and her mother over there, and just watch for a moment to notice how they are with each other now." (I kept saying "now" because I wanted some part of Loreen's inner mind to connect what we were doing to the present moment at the same time as she was reframing her experience of herself in the past.)

As she watched, Loreen felt that she noticed a new connection between the mother and the little girl, more closeness, more warmth, more tenderness: "I am aware of how close they are together, with happier faces, warmer feelings."

Profoundly light-hearted strategies for unsticking stuck stuff

Then I asked her to return to the present moment, be in her present body, bringing all these feelings and learnings into this moment here and now, "letting them just fill your knowing of who you are now."

I asked her to just check inside and notice if there was any part of her that would object to just having these loving feelings all the time, like we have with something so natural as breathing?

After a moment of reflection, Loreen said that there was a "rigorous critical part" of her that was very suspicious of all this. Was this really happening? How, it wanted to know, can you measure whether something is really going on?

I said that having a physical body was a great measuring device! I asked her to remember how she had felt (and still was feeling), filled up with warm radiant love, and to acknowledge that that had been a real feeling. I suggested that she invite that critical part to notice how easy it was to calibrate the level of the feelings she was noticing actually in her body. What did it think of that?

In the end, Loreen's critical part acknowledged that "even for as amorphous a feeling as love, it is still possible - in a not so rigorous but OK way - to tell when you have got more, or less, of that feeling, and how much you are able to feel. I realize I can use my own body as a guidepost."

With this perspective, her critical side was willing to accept that there was a way to actually measure of whether something was "really happening, or really true."

Our time was almost up for this session, but I suggested that another time we might do the same work with her memory of her father. Or she might feel inspired to explore the memories of her father herself, making sure she remembered to use EFT for anything that came up that was uncomfortable. Loreen said goodbye, still feeling the warm glow of goodness and love in her, and knowing that she could return to that feeling any time. It is a memory for her now.

Whenever we do this ancestral healing work of helping the universe to hold a little light in a heart that was previously felt dark, it helps all of us.

We are **born** good enough!

The more of our love and goodness that we can actually experience in ourselves, the more love and goodness there is available everywhere, even across time and space.

Profoundly light-hearted strategies for unsticking stuck stuff

10
YOU ARE
STRONG
& COURAGEOUS!

Something Deeper at Work!

George's Story
Why don't we do what's right for ourselves?

Because we are so smart and capable (even if we don't believe that) and so little understood, the theme of many sensitive people's lives becomes "I have to tough it out."

George is a bright young man who came to free himself of an annoying habit, although it turned out that chronic pain was his real issue. We weren't having much success.

I figured that he was about to say thanks, I knew it wouldn't work, see you, so I began to say I was sorry that we had not made more progress with his problem, and that I hadn't been able to help more.

"Oh no!" he said. "I like coming here and I look forward to it!" That got my attention. Why was he liking coming to see me

Profoundly light-hearted strategies for unsticking stuck stuff

if we weren't making progress? There must be something else going on here, I thought.

I began to probe deeper, suspecting that the pain might be a clue (he hadn't mentioned it to me - his wife had, when she made the appointment for him). But when I brought it up he said, "Oh, that is a whole other can of worms. There is nothing I can do about that."

Going deeper....

Curious, I asked when the pain started. "In graduate school," he said. What was his experience of graduate school, I asked?

"Hate and misery," he said at once, his body hunching.

Oh.

He'd tried many different doctors, treatments, and approaches, getting little relief. Acupuncture helped, but the results weren't lasting.

Nothing seems to work!

It seemed that finally he had determined that nothing would work and he would just have to adapt to a life of increasing pain in his muscles and joints. He hadn't been evaluated for fibromyalgia but it sounded to me like he was on his way.

Very athletic, his strategy had been to do more and more physical activity, stretching his limits further and further, always dogged by a debilitating competitive performance anxiety.

He was at the top of his sports, his body would be exhausted, his fingernails were in bloody shreds from nervous picking, he was increasingly in pain - but he wasn't having to think about what he was doing and why.

Introducing EFT

I asked if he would humor me by trying some EFT with the pain. He gave his lower back pain a 4 (I thought that was underestimating it). (See chapter 11)

We tapped for fairly general things: "this pain," "the emotions that might be connected to this pain," and to his surprise the pain diminished. He looked quite bemused.

Then we began to go deeper with likely connected emotional issues, and the pain increased.

"This always happens...."

I could see his mind clicking through his options. At last he said, "This is what always happens. It is just not going to work. But that's OK. I can tough it out."

"Soldier on. Hunker down." I said. He was nodding.

I realized that there was a deeper paradigm at work.

Unconsciously, I believed, he had adopted this "tough it out, I can handle it" life view in order to avoid thinking about and feeling the true conflict going on inside of him.

In spite of the emotional pain he was feeling, he had gone on to finish graduate school because "that's the only way I can get a good job in my field."

And he stayed working in his rather boring "good" job now

because "I have to support my family and the baby on the way." When the pain began showing up in his joints (can we say flexibility?) he could focus on that, rather than the "hate and misery."

I can tough it out!

I told George I thought there was some good work that we could do together, but that doing it would probably provoke some deep change.

There was a part of him that was frightened by this, resisting it. I wanted to let that part of him know that I didn't intend to kill it off – I just wanted to find better, more effective ways for it to get what it was trying to get for him, a happy heart, however he manifested it.

Appealing to his intelligence and ability to engage in some thoughtful exchange, I offered more sessions of just exploring "life paradigms" with interest and curiosity. I wanted to reassure that wary part of him that I was really on its side, not an enemy. He left, saying he would think about it.

I found myself telling George's story to other clients (keeping his name and details anonymous). It was such a good illustration of how we tend to fall into a "tough it out" life paradigm, creating an identity around it, forgetting how to honor what is deepest in us.

Andrea's Story

*When I explained my idea about the "tough it out" paradigm to Andrea, she asked what the word **paradigm** meant.*

Andrea is a woman in her early 40's who has never believed in herself.

She has a lot of experience in building structures with her hands, so I likened a paradigm to the structure of a house.

Acknowledging that I had no experience building a house, still I had noticed that the first step is to build a foundation, and then to erect a structure of wood, sort of like a skeleton that the house's body is then built around. That wooden frame, I said, is like a paradigm.

We have all constructed an internal, largely unconscious frame of thought and belief that functions as a structure in and around which we build our lives

The Rescuer
For Andrea, her paradigm is about being a competent caretaker.

Her childhood was emotionally bleak, scary, threatened, uncertain. She spent years trying to rescue her mother.

After getting sober, she has been a devoted caretaker of other, apparently less competent people, trying to make the world a safe place for them. Unconsciously she is trying to make a safe world for herself.

She understood this explanation of "paradigm" right away. And she got the connection with the pain and exhaustion she was beginning to feel in her body. Doing for others can take its toll.

In another session

Andrea found some major relief from almost-lifelong back pain. The backstory was about neglect - of herself as a child, of her by herself now, of feeling that she had to take care of her partner's health first, by working a job that had good partner health benefits - even though doing this job was taking a great toll on her own health.

Andrea feels very strongly about taking an honorable stance and keeping her commitments. Her very survival as a child rested upon doing as she was told and being super reliable... though of course nothing she did was ever good enough.

I finally got her to start dreaming (just dreaming, not thinking, couldn't go there) of doing different work, and she began to make a list of what she might like.

She was really getting into the list when she said, "...and someone to take care of ME...." Then suddenly - "OW!!!"

At the very moment that she said, "someone to take care of ME," Andrea got this terrible pain in her back! We cleared that, using EFT with the realization that she had a deep seated belief that nobody could/would take care of her - she had to do it all herself.

And then she became aware of this other, deeper pain, that she has had since she was a child. It apparently had come from a back injury, but as Nancy Selfridge said earlier in these pages, those do heal. This one was about the ongoing and connected emotional pain.

Andrea has to lift a lot at her job, but had felt she had to lie about her back pain to get the job in the first place. Now it seemed as though this deeper pain was where the accumulated childhood neglect was still living.

She had thought there was no way to change that pain, she'd just have to live with it (tough it out...). We worked with this pain too with EFT. That night she called me, amazed, to say she still felt fine, for the first time in decades!

Update!

Andrea called not long ago, announcing very proudly, "I just wanted to let you know that I'm doing well and standing strong!"

NOTES

11
LEARN AND USE EFT

What *is* EFT?

EFT is a rapid, highly effective, easy-to-learn self-healing technique.

Remember this, first and foremost:

All chronic pain - whether physical, emotional or mental - is about the story we tell ourselves about our experience

I teach people an easy-to-learn method of dissolving anxiety and stress, easing both physical and emotional pain, releasing fears and negative or limiting beliefs of any kind. It is based on five thousand years of practical study in Chinese Medicine about the way the energy system of the body is affected by negative emotion.

This method works literally in a matter of minutes, replacing emotional distress with a form of peace, calm or confidence.

This remarkable and refreshing new approach is called Emotional Freedom Techniques (EFT). In essence it is like yoga for the emotions and the spirit, or a psychological version of acupuncture except that needles aren't necessary.

EFT involves tapping gently on the stress relief points of the body with the fingertips, places we instinctively touch or rub anyway when we are upset, like around the eyes and on the chest.

Features

✳ The results are usually long lasting.
✳ The process is relatively gentle.
✳ Most people can apply the techniques to themselves.
✳ It is inexpensive to learn and use, and easy to teach in a group while still maintaining individual privacy.
✳ It often provides relief for physical and emotional pain, headaches and addictive cravings.

Where it has been useful

EFT has been proven clinically effective in the Veterans Administration with many of our Vietnam War Veterans. It has helped in weight-loss programs and has also assisted students with "learning blocks."

EFT has provided noticeable gains in many performance areas such as sports, music and public speaking. Those who meditate find that EFT allows them to "go deeper" and mental health professionals are reporting dramatic improvements in their clients' well being.

For more information

EFT does not do everything for everyone and is still in the experimental stage. However, the clinical results over the last 5 years have been remarkable. For more information, visit the EFT web site at: www.emofree.com

This is wonderful healing work that is easy to learn, highly effective, and an empowering self care tool that puts the ability to clear your path toward inner peace literally into your own hands.

I think it is best to get started by working with an accomplished practitioner for a time to get experience and a sense of how to use these techniques creatively for greatest effectiveness. From there, you can heal your own life.

"EFT is astonishing both in its simplicity and its effectiveness in dislodging and removing emotional hurts and painful memories. I have found it powerful in healing present-time emotional pain (self hatred and self rejection) and in removing the hurt of events long past.

"I experienced liberation from difficult childhood experiences, and not only was the past healed, but I was empowered through the process so that my current habits of better self care were reinforced and strengthened." (quote from a client)

The idea that, by using EFT, we can take greater responsibility for our own emotional and physical well-being is more than exciting!

The EFT Process: *(diagrams start on page 93)*

The set-up statement:

A. Say statements 1 - 3 in a complete set three times as you strike the Karate Chop Point:

> *1.* Even though I ____(insert your phrase here)____

> *2.* I deeply and completely accept myself (or, if for a child: I'm a great kid, or another appropriate phrase)

> *3.* and I choose _____(insert your phrase here)____

The Tapping Sequence:

B. Repeat the reminder phrase (the gist of the Even Though statement) as you tap on the face and body

C. Repeat the reminder, or "I choose" phrase as you tap down the points on the face and body

An example:

A. Striking the Karate Chop Point:
> *1.* Even though I can't sleep
> *2.* I deeply and completely accept myself
> *3.* And I choose to sleep well and wake up refreshed

B. Tapping the issue:
> Repeat "can't sleep," "can't sleep," etc., as you tap on the points. Do two rounds minimum; do more if necessary

C. Tapping the choice:

> Repeat "sleep well," "awaken refreshed," "sleep well," "awaken refreshed," etc., as you tap on the points on the face and body.

Do a minimum of two rounds tapping; do more if it feels right. Add the Finger Points and/or The Gamut for stubborn issues.

On the following pages you will find illustrations of the various tapping points.

Of these points, the most commonly referred to are the Karate Chop Point, the Sore Spots, and the Main Tapping Points.

You will also see the Finger Points, the Gamut, and the Prosperity Procedure.

Enjoy, and tap on everything!

Profoundly light-hearted strategies for unsticking stuck stuff

Tapping Tips

The Karate Chop Point:

While it's OK to use the Karate Chop Point of either hand, it's usually most convenient to tap the Karate Chop Point of the non-dominant hand with the two fingertips of the dominant hand.

For example, if you are right handed, you would tap the Karate Chop Point on your left hand with the fingertips of your right hand.

Tapping intensity:

Tap solidly but never so hard as to hurt or bruise yourself.

Tapping and counting:

Tap about 7 times on each one of the tapping points. Because it might be difficult to count at the same time you repeat your phrases as you tap, if you are a little over or a little under 7 (5 to 9, for example) that will be usually be sufficient.

The points:

Each energy meridian has two end points. You need only tap on one end to balance out disruptions that may exist in it. These end points are near the surface of the body and are thus more readily accessed than other points along the energy meridians that may be more deeply buried.

Points on both sides of the body:

Most of the tapping points exist on either side of the body. It doesn't matter which side you use, nor does it matter if you switch sides during the sequence. For example, you can tap under your right eye and, later in the sequence, tap under your left arm.

Which hand?

It's OK to tap with either hand but most people prefer to use their dominant hand (i.e.: your right hand if you are right handed).

Tap with the fingertips of your index finger and second finger. This covers a larger area than just tapping with one fingertip, and allows you to cover the tapping points more easily.

excerpted from Gary Craig's EFT Course

Learn how to use EFT, and apply it to the many situations and symptoms of pain, fear, illness, and anxiety you may have in your life. Use it to create a new and better life for yourself!

Go forth and **prosper!**

NOTES

Profoundly light-hearted strategies for unsticking stuck stuff

THE KARATE CHOP POINT

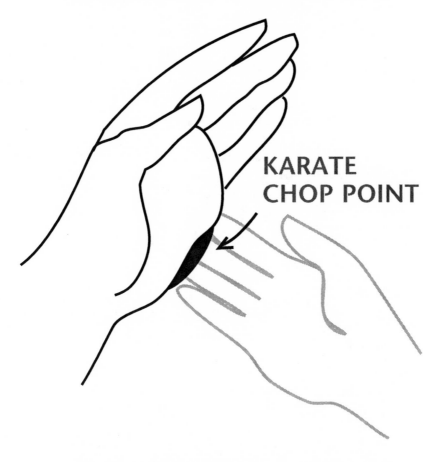

KARATE
CHOP POINT

strike the Karate Chop Point gently with either the tips of the first two fingers or the inside of the combined flattened fingers of the other hand

Profoundly light-hearted strategies for unsticking stuck stuff

THE TAPPING SPOTS

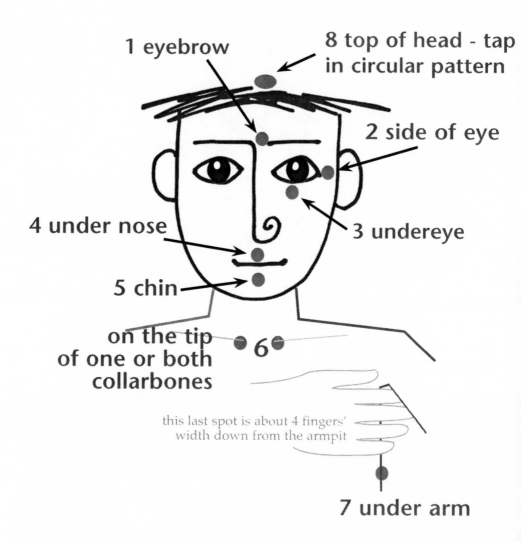

1 eyebrow

8 top of head - tap in circular pattern

2 side of eye

4 under nose

3 undereye

5 chin

on the tip of one or both collarbones 6

this last spot is about 4 fingers' width down from the armpit

7 under arm

THE FINGER POINTS

Use these points with the Gamut point to pack more WOW into your session!

points are right at the edge of the fingernails

Karate Chop Point

Starting at the side of the thumbnail nearest you, then tap on the spot right next to the nail on the edge of the fingernail on each finger *except* the ring finger.

End up tapping on the Karate Chop Point.

© Rue Hass 2005 ✳ 97 ✳ IntuitiveMentoring.com
Profoundly light-hearted strategies for unsticking stuck stuff

THE GAMUT

Add this step after tapping the face & body, and/or Finger Points. It helps put the body and brain back into balance.

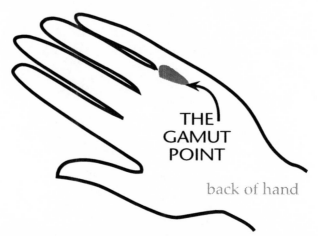

THE
GAMUT
POINT

back of hand

Rub the Gamut Spot (the V-shaped indentation on the back of the hand at the base of the knuckles of 3rd and 4th fingers) as you go through these steps:

*Looking straight forward (but relaxed!)
and keeping your head **still**:*

1. Close the eyes
2. Open the eyes
3. Look down *(eyes move only!)* to the hard left
4. Look down *(eyes move only!)* to the hard right
5. Still without moving the head, do a wide rotation of the eyes in one direction 360 degrees
6. Do a wide rotation of the eyes in the other direction 360 degrees
7. Hum a few notes of a tune (like happy birthday to you)
8. Count from one to five
9. Hum a few notes of a tune

Profoundly light-hearted strategies for unsticking stuck stuff

THE TEMPORAL TAP
FOR PROSPERITY

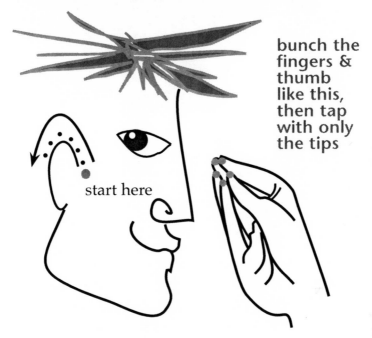

bunch the fingers & thumb like this, then tap with only the tips

start here

Bunch the tips of the thumb and fingers together.
Start to tap where the right ear *(the right ear only!)*
leaves its connection to the face.
Tap right next to the ear, but not on the ear.
Do three rounds of: tapping up and around the ear,
ending halfway down the back down behind the ear
(as shown above), repeating this statement
(or a version you like better):

I graciously accept good, joy and prosperity into my life, and all my needs are abundantly met, now and always.

Prosperity Phrasing by Michelle Hardwick

Profoundly light-hearted strategies for unsticking stuck stuff

THIS IS WHERE I STAND

NOTES

12
LIVE FROM YOUR OWN RULES!

Sick and Tired of Trying to Follow "Unknown Rules"

Ann's Story

Ann came in saying she was sick, AGAIN, for the third time in a few weeks, and this time it seemed to have been triggered by a dream.

She has been battling with a stressful job, a tendency to over-perform at home, and recent tests to determine if her breast cancer has returned.

After she awakened from this dream her fibromyalgia symptoms were raging, especially pain in her face and in her legs and knees.

I asked Ann what title she would give to her dream. She said, "Oh, I'm not good at titles," and then said, "It could be 'What the Heck Happened?'"

In her dream, she had arrived at work one day at her management job in a large corporation.

She has risen to this level in recognition of her creativity, intuition, and her ability to problem-solve and create ingenious solutions for her company.

Ever since the successful and supportive local firm she worked for was acquired by a large national corporation, it has felt to her like she is "working for the <X brand> mafia," and her skills seem much less valued in favor of a more linear, macho business culture.

Even though she continues to receive excellent evaluations, Ann has begun to feel a lot of anxiety and self-doubt.

A message
So in the dream she arrives at work and hears a message on her voicemail from one of the authority figures in her company, a "mafia" type she feels very uncomfortable around.

What have I done wrong?

When her recorded message said her name, this man responded, "Ann Talbott? You're not Ann Talbott. You don't work here anymore."

She hung up, frozen with worry and self-recrimination, wondering what had caused this, what had she done wrong, what are people thinking about her, what should she do?

Profoundly light-hearted strategies for unsticking stuck stuff

No support

In the dream she goes home looking for support from her husband, and finds him outside next to a line of big, noisy semi trucks waiting for something to do.

She feels he is too busy to pay attention to her. So she goes back inside, feeling judged and rejected, but with a slowly growing sense that maybe she should fight this.

Working with dreams

Dreamwork fits in really well with EFT, producing a wealth of set up phrases and physiology to notice and tap for.

It also elicits a path of communication with the other, less conscious, parts of the mind that are speaking to us through our dreams - often with a clear message of a new and healing direction to take (I learned this technique years ago in my Neuro-Linguistic Programming training from Tiana Galgano. I use this dream work myself, as well as using it in my spiritual counseling/coaching practice. There are lots of ways to practice).

Condensing the dream

I asked Ann to label a few key frames that would be the highlights or most intense moments.

(As I wrote the above, my husband, who was reading over my shoulder, suggested that this is like a DVD of a movie that has "Scene Selections." He showed me a flyer that comes with a movie he has that has exactly this kind of list of frames with titles. Great idea!)

Tuning in

Next I invited Ann to take each frame and feel into the emotions and body feelings that were in it, to just consider each frame as if it were an intuitive message, in and of itself, not thinking particularly about her life or the whole dream, and say what came to mind.

In each of these different "tunings-in" I was jotting down her words and phrases in a grid system I have developed for myself to make note-taking easier.

Dialing in

Feeling: normal	*Message:* This is my life

"ANN TALBOTT? You're not ANN TALBOTT!"

Feeling: Shock	*Message:* Rug pulled out from under me, my foundation shifted

"You don't work here any more"

Feeling: Frozen, my stomach drops, legs weak, can't move	*Message:* You are not who you think you are. You are not the person who does this job.

Profoundly light-hearted strategies for unsticking stuck stuff

THIS IS WHERE I STAND

"What caused it? What should I do?"

Feeling: Embarrassed, feeling judged, judging myself, I wasn't good enough	*Message:* I don't know what I will do next

Husband next to trucks

Feeling: lonely, sad, abandoned, rejected	*Message:* He is too busy. He won't pay attention to me. I have no support from him.

Go back in

Feeling: Confused	*Message:* I don't know what I will do next

"Maybe I should fight this"

Feeling: courage and confidence coming back	*Message:* I can stand up for myself. I can seek out my connections and my own support

Dream it again!

Following this, I asked Ann to go back into the dream and "re-dream" it from the point of view or perspective of each of the characters or objects in the dream, as if each character and

Profoundly light-hearted strategies for unsticking stuck stuff

object were a part of her that had its own insights to offer. Each time she would report back whatever thoughts or images or feelings came to mind. This sounded weird to her, but she was able to do it without any trouble. Here are my notes of what she said:

Paul (the Mafia manager)
> "I'm going to get rid of her. Put my guys in there."

Telephone system
> My job is to pass on information, to get my messages heard

Husband
> I realize that he actually didn't see me. He is doing a job that is beneath his capabilities. He is not very happy doing this. I notice that he has a cup in his hand – he has only a small amount to give in this situation. He is going to give it to the truck drivers.

Trucks
> They are powerful potential energy, waiting for a job. They are not very happy doing this job. They are just doing it for a living.

Drivers
> They are lined up, ready to go, waiting to go somewhere.

Messages about your life

Finally, I read all these comments from the grid and the re-dreaming back to Ann, as if they were "just" messages, not about the dream but about her life.

I asked her to listen to them in this way, objectively, as an observer. As you are reading this yourself, you might go back and do the same thing. When I did this, the message from Ann's inner self seemed abundantly clear.

Clarity

She thought so too, and she was really shocked at the clarity of what she was hearing. When I asked her to put together what she heard, Ann said, "I have been having all these physical symptoms, migraines, fibromyalgia pain, illness, dozing off – I can't seem to stay awake! – to say nothing about the stress of the cancer tests.

"I can see so clearly now how my symptoms can come from the emotions I don't even realize that I am feeling. The dream is showing me what I am really feeling.

I am sleeping through my life!

"And what I am really feeling is that I am in such pain from unconsciously trying to live from 'unknown rules.' Like 'they' know something I don't and they are always judging me for not measuring up. I am internalizing those judgments so I am always judging myself. I feel all the time like I am in a falling elevator."

I'm always judging myself

I mentioned that except for the voicemail system and herself, all the characters and props in her dream were male. It was as if all the masculine energy in her - her power - was being held back, limited, or utilized in a small and unfulfilling way, waiting to be given something to do, waiting for meaning.

A surprise reconnection

It had occurred to Ann in this process that she wanted to renew the connection she has with her best friend from the past, amazingly also named Ann, who is equally creative and sensitive and very supportive, and with whom she used to work. Together, they had developed the new systems that have served their pre-acquisition employer so well, and upon which our Ann's good reputation at work are based.

They lost touch when the other Ann left this company and moved to Chicago. I thought it was so interesting to hear our Ann say, "I need to reconnect with Ann," as if the friend Ann represents an alter-ego who embodies all the dormant creative abilities that are going unrecognized and underutilized by the culture of the company as it has evolved after the take-over by the "<brand x> mafia."

I asked Ann what the opposite of living from unknown rules is

She said without hesitation:
Living from my own rules!

Profoundly light-hearted strategies for unsticking stuck stuff

Next time we get together we will incorporate all the different information we elicited from the dream into tapping set-ups, ending with a *Choices* set-up (*see the work of Pat Carrington at EFTupdate.com*) of something like "I choose now to discover how creative, supportive and satisfying it is to live from my own rules." She can also tap on all these realizations at home.

Probably Ann is not quite ready to actually quit her job yet, but perhaps that time is coming, and she has already begun to tune into ways of living that honor her own sovereignty.

NOTES

Profoundly light-hearted strategies for unsticking stuck stuff

13
YOU ARE IMPORTANT!

"They treated me like a non-person so I grew up treating myself like a non-person."

Gina's Story

Coincidentally, the very day I did the work with Ann, I got an email from a former student in one of the fibromyalgia classes I taught with Dr. Nancy Selfridge.

Gina is a creative, sensitive, gifted and talented woman who has been virtually (and literally) killing herself all her life working as an accountant, a job she is good at but which she hates.

Dear Rue,

The timing of your e-mail (announcing the next Freedom From Fibromyalgia class) was amazing.

I just moments ago gave my notice.
I'm done with this job as of Jan 21st.

There is no doubt in my mind that my work with you was a major factor in my ability to make this decision.

Thank you.

Love,

Gina

When I thanked **her**, and asked if I could quote her, she said...

Absolutely, you may quote me and use my name.

I have to admit I'm terrified about what I'll do next.

I'm banking on the adage, "When God closes one door, he always opens a window."

Thank you for all of your wonderful support and love. I swear sometimes I felt you sending me good wishes.

Thanks for your love & blessings.

Gina Pate

NOTE: Her given name is Georgia, but in our class she took to calling herself by her karaoke stage name "Gina." She is a gifted singer whose talent was purposefully not acknowledged or fostered by her family.

Gina talked about her experience of growing up in a family that didn't notice, honor, and even value her sensitivity. In fact, it is probably more true to say that one or both of her parents *were* sensitive, but had shut down their feelings to protect themselves from a lifetime of pain and unfulfilled dreams of their own.

If we could look into their deepest heart for their positive intention behind what looked and felt to Gina like abuse and neglect (and it was!), we would find that they were thinking unconsciously that their actions were protecting her from a similar life of pain.

Through their attitudes and unconscious behavior, they were telling her:

"Don't get your hopes up, kid –
it is a hard world out there."
"You got to be tough to make it."
"I am doing this for your own good."

So REALLY, deep inside, they were acting out of love for her. But that is not the message Gina got. Just like her parents had not gotten that message from those very same actions by their own parents. And it goes back and back. In some way that we can't understand, the healing work we do with EFT is healing both the past and the future.

Gina continues...

People say to me, why do you let things bother you? You get upset so easily!

Someone told me that after I decided to leave my job. "Why not let it roll off your back," she added.

And I thought to myself, "Well how good are *you* at that? You think you have no problems. Yet you have allergies, asthma, other physical conditions – do you really think there is no correlation?"

I was always sensitive to bright lights, big crowds, loud music. And I LOVE music. I don't like being around lots of people. I am very hermit like.

I know I must have been incredibly sensitive as a child. There were many emotional traumas in my life.

I never felt like I had much of a voice in speaking my mind. That has caused me problems in my life. I have very decided opinions, but had no voice as a child.

My father believed that children should be seen and not heard

From ages 14 to 16 I was really drawn to abstract thought, philosophical things, religion - maybe philosophy more than religion - more than most people I knew in school, but I never had opportunity to express it at home.

At school I was so bored

Ever since I started doing the EFT tapping work with you I have come to realize I am smarter and more perceptive, more intuitive than I ever knew I was. I know things. I read my husband's mind all the time. I beam stuff out to him.

I have come to realize
I am smarter and more perceptive,
more intuitive than I ever knew I was

I have always been exceptionally sensitive to music – at 11, I saw *West Side Story* and cried because the music was so beautiful. People would say, "What's the matter?" Singing could bring me to tears.

I didn't get a chance!

My parents were tired of being parents. They didn't encourage the girls to do anything. In grade school my teacher said I could sing, but I didn't get a chance.

My parents said, "Oh, yeah, that's nice," but I was not encouraged to do anything. The irony is that my father was in show business as an acrobatic performer – he loved being in front of a crowd, but he never saw that in me.

I remember my parents had people over one night when I was 10 or 11. They had me come out of my room and sing a song. They said, "That was wonderful, now go back to your bedroom." That was the only time they ever encouraged me.

I really wanted to learn guitar. My mother said, "Oh, your sister and brother took that but they didn't like it. I'm sure you won't either."

I convinced her to get me a guitar, and then asked if I could get lessons. I was told, "You never stick to anything. You have to prove to me that you're not going to waste our money on lessons."

I just took it in that the fault was me

Ten years later my mother said, "See, I told you so!" when the guitar gathered dust. But how did they expect me to maintain interest if they never let me learn?

I don't think my mother wanted me to have anything she didn't have

I stayed in my accounting job WAY past when I should have left. I should never even have done that work. I was good at it, but I was bored by it, and no one ever encouraged me to think I was worth doing anything else.

When I began a couple of years ago to look at why I was in so much pain, I felt anger at myself for not having figured out how to let go of that job. I was sad that I am sad.

Now that I have quit I have to be careful , thinking I have no right to be angry and sad any more. I feel guilty if I am not happy and blissful that I am no longer in that job. I have to be up and happy and chipper for my husband.

It made me angry that I couldn't tough it out

I kept thinking I should be able to do this

Not being able to tough it out would be a failure, a sign of weakness I should be able to let it roll off, not let it bother me. That is a philosophy I was raised with.

If you got hurt, you would hear "Oh, you're not that badly hurt, just tough it out." That carried into emotions too. I didn't tell my dad I had quit my job because I was afraid he would see me as a failure.

But I knew in my heart that the failure would be to stay

I get frustrated that my body won't do what I want it to do without hurting. I can't push myself like my father can. Literally he can work circles around me. He has a toughness. He just overcomes the body.

I'm me, not my father!
Now I know that the sensitive temperament requires that you pay attention to the body!

I can stand back and look at my body as a separate entity. I find myself talking to it: "Why can't you work better!" I will work to exhaustion. There is so much to do. I never thought about it until I started doing this healing work, but I realize that those are not real healthy beliefs to maintain.

With all this pain, my body must be saying "You need to give me more rest, not have such high expectations!"

When I get rid of anger
I feel more relaxed

I hold anger, tension in my body as a coiled spring. When I tap I can literally feel the tenseness draining out of me and I can breathe and relax.

The other thing that tapping really does for me is saying "I deeply and completely accept myself." That has had a profound effect on my own sense of value.

I have come to appreciate myself, recognize myself, my own intelligence

Tapping gets this knowing into my belief system. It gets into your cells somehow.

I think I always knew I was intelligent but I didn't want anyone to know. I wasn't capable of acknowledging that because that is being proud, conceited.

14
THEY CALLED ME CRYBABY!

Stand up for yourself!

Madelyn's Story
Madelyn is a successful, dynamic executive in a large corporation.

My sensitivity started as a child, being sensitive emotionally to things, getting my feelings hurt easily. My family called me a crybaby a lot.

One of your parents calling you a crybaby – that is not a good feeling. I got spanked when I was little. At the time spanking was a common way of raising children. But for me it was way too intense.

I was so sensitive that they only would have had to look at me cross-eyed to upset me

I don't remember having thought that I got what I deserved.

Probably what came out of that for me was a belief in being unsafe, never knowing when things would blow up. I wasn't a rebellious kid.

When I look at my father, I think he had it. He had a very big startle reflex, a hair-trigger temper. He would startle first, and then be very mad. It was scary for me.

We moved twice in my high school years to different cities. As a sensitive person you need to grow up with a close circle of friends,and feel like you have a group.

But I feel that to go to a whole new group twice stunted me a little. I am not the kind of person who can go up to a table full of kids in the cafeteria and say "Hi, I'm new, can I eat with you?"

As I grew up, being sensitive manifested as being a good friend to people, but liking small groups rather than large groups. Because you can make deeper connections.

More sensitive to pain
I always thought I was sensitive to the senses more than other people, and then when I found out later that I had fibromyalgia, I looked back and could see that I was already more sensitive to pain early in my life. For example, in high school I would have to spend a couple days in bed with menstrual cramps.

Escalating pain
In my 20s, I continued to escalate with physical symptoms that were suggesting, if I had known how to know this, that something was way out of balance.

I started out with spastic colon, and then problems with sleep from stress at work, and I got worse.

I kept going up the mountain with my symptoms, and then having a plateau, 'til I hit the next level with breast cancer. That was Pikes Peak. I found a lump in my breast in 2001. That added the emotional stress, and the physical stress of chemo and radiation.

My sensitivity gives me access to creativity

I have been exceptionally successful both in school and at work. My sensitivity gives me access to creativity. I have an ability to sense, or pick up what it is that people need, and turn that into a creative solution. That is a positive thing.

And my sensitivity makes me a really good mom.

Something you said to me, Rue, about sensitive people being like the canary the miners used - I know I pick up stuff before others do. I like to use that at work to help make the place better for everybody.

Planning for less pain

I am a planner and a perfectionist. You have to do so much planning to accommodate sensitivity, make sure you are not in situations that you can't take care of.

My husband took me to a concert recently for my birthday. It was so loud physically that I felt assaulted by the sound waves. It was so hard to see all 800 of the other people there having a good time. That was a pain in the butt.

One of the major things is trying to avoid getting my feelings hurt and avoid that whole "freeze" situation I get into. Over the years as those situations come up, I have learned from them too well – I always try to *plan* my way out of getting into those situations again. The cage just gets smaller.

Planning never works!!!
I am learning that
you can't think yourself out of this

When I look back at things that happened to me that had a negative impact, one experience I remember is when we were in 6th grade all lined up to go back in after playground.

There was a girl – she *had* been my best friend, but also she was the queen bee. One day she decided that she didn't like me, and proceeded to tell me how much she hated me in front of other kids. That kind of queen bee person recognizes the sensitive ones and uses them as a target.

Now what did I do?!?
The other imprint was in junior high. The 8th graders had a tradition of mentoring 7th graders. I had a party for my fellow 7th graders early in the school year.

The next night at the football stadium, a couple of 8th grade girls dressed me up and down in front of everybody for hating the 8th graders. I didn't know that the older grade was supposed to mentor the younger grade, and anyway they must not have been doing a very good job of it because I hadn't known! I was devastated.

It always seems like there are Unwritten Rules. Even now, today, I am always trying to see them, PLAN for them, so I won't trip over them. But that is the whole thing about unwritten rules –- you can't see them.

"How do you stand up for yourself?"

Weak in the knees
One day Madelyn came into my office feeling "weak in the knees, a hurt, numb buzzy feeling."

When she was sitting down, the intensity of the sensation was a 3 out of 10, but standing up, it was a 7. She said, "It feels like I want to collapse - you know, the feeling you get before you are about to faint."

She's a business consultant, and she talked about having gone recently to a client meeting on the East Coast.

Traveling had been a nightmare - cancelled and rescheduled planes and missed connections, people at the other end left hanging, and in addition to the stress of the journey she was feeling guilty and mad at herself because she had turned responsibility for the trip over to her colleague, who she had seen as a seasoned traveler. But he turned out to not be as aware as he might have been, hence their difficulties.

Madelyn started feeling dizzy and weak-kneed right there in the airport, and those feelings increased over the challenging next few days of the scheduled meetings. She was able to stuff her usual feelings of frustration and inadequacy for the duration of the meetings, but she said, "I paid later."

I stuffed my feelings, but paid the price later!

When she began talking about an upcoming meeting where she feared she would be asked to take on a major national project, the discomfort in her knees went up to "at least an 8 out of ten."

Madelyn is a very successful, high achieving perfectionist, inclined to "push through" whatever she is feeling to get the job done right.

She is actually a highly sensitive introvert, if she were being who she really is, which she hasn't been. As a result, not surprisingly, she has suffered from fibromyalgia for many years, and also had breast cancer two years ago.

On her return from the earlier meeting, she went to a physical therapist who does myofascial release for her knees. The Physical Therapist had said that her fascia is always tight in that area, and in fact all over her body.

I went to work with the knees, using EFT set-up phrases. We repeated: "these weak knees," "hurt, numb and buzzing knees," "these wanting to collapse knees." Her intensity rating went down by one point.

I asked Madelyn to say more about feeling weakness in her knees: "What is bringing you to your knees?"

She started talking about another upcoming national meeting, where she was afraid they were going to ask her to take the lead on a major project, and she just didn't feel "up" to doing that. Not enough "down" time, she would "end 'up' in pain," "I'm not good at relating to all those 'up' sales guys," "I don't think well on my feet." I'm starting to notice a pattern here....

I really should....
What will people think?
I'm just a wimp....

She went on, saying that she felt she didn't have any choice, she really should lead this project, she hadn't told anyone about the fibromyalgia (and wouldn't have told anyone about the cancer - she was planning to get right back to work after surgery, but then was forced to tell people about the chemotherapy). "What will people think?" "They will think I am wimping out."

These were excellent phrases to use in the set-up and on the tapping points. Her intensity went down to a 5.

Thinking about the physiological and metaphorical role of knees, we began to talk about standing up for herself, speaking up for herself, how hard that was for her.

"I'm not good at asking for what I need, asking to be heard.

It feels like I am 'hollering into the night and no one is there.'"

"But," she said, "I am finding that overachieving doesn't bring the same satisfaction that it used to."

I was wondering out loud how we could reframe and work with the idea of standing up for yourself. What actually holds you up? How could you reframe using your knees for holding yourself "up"? What did her knees want for her by wanting to fall "down," and hurting when she wasn't standing "up" for what was really true for her?

We fell into one of those serendipitous conversational flows that seem to come when you open yourself to your intuition and wonder out loud and internally about something, and I got a great insight into fibromyalgia:

All her life, Madelyn had been forcing herself to do things she didn't feel comfortable with, and had developed a kind of *rigid forcing tension* throughout her body that became very painful.

Unresolved emotional pain and trauma turns into actual physical tightness

The pain came from *chronically tense muscles,* held in a protective, defensive readiness, which had led to contracted, tight, stiff fascia all over her body, creating constant pain.

Fascia is the tough, connective tissue web between the skin and the body's underlying structure of muscle and bone (it's what you see if you skin a raw chicken – that almost transparent sheet between the skin and the muscle).

Ordinarily, most of us don't ever even think of the fascia - we think about bones, muscle, fat, organs. But the fascia is an incredibly important part of the body - it surrounds every organ, duct, nerve, blood vessel, muscle and bone. Strong? Fascia has a tensile strength of over 2,000 pounds per square inch. And what's of paramount importance is that it can become severely bound by shock, trauma and stress.

Unresolved emotional pain and trauma turns into physical tightness in the body. As the fascia tightens, the body must work harder and harder just to perform daily activities, leading to fatigue and *feeling very like depression.*

The fascia can become severely bound by shock, trauma and stress

Medical Intuitive Carolyn Myss has said that "our biography becomes our biology." Neuroscientist Bessel van der Kolk says, "The body keeps the score." It occurred to me that the fascia is one of the scoreboards for the body.

"The body keeps the score"

My armor

Together, tapping and talking, Madelyn and I created an image of the fascia as having become a painful suit of armor that was trying to hold her up - reflecting all of the limiting beliefs that she carried about who she felt she must be in the world to succeed: the "I should's," "I have to's," " I have no choice," "What will they think of me if I don't _____," all the pushing toward perfection and performance.

The fascia is meant to *support*, not hold us up!

Tap tap tap… "this painful suit of armor… trying to help me stand up for myself… trying to protect me from being hurt, ignored, rejected… holding my Self tightly to keep it safe… this painful suit of armor in my knees…"

What else would work better?

As we continued using EFT to tap, sometimes pausing on one point or another to talk, I asked Madelyn what would work better as a support for holding her up? And where would she feel that in her body?

She said, *"It would be a feeling that I can just freely connect with others, and open to a flow of love and affection, letting that flow out to others and feeling it flow back into me, no longer feeling separate from them."*

She felt this in her chest, as movement and flow going out and returning.

Tapping on the karate chop point, we walked through feeling a free-flowing connection with people she loved, and then moved into experiencing the flow with others who were more challenging, even those "up" salesmen.

I don't want to use my cancer as an excuse

Suddenly she said, "When I go to that meeting, I really can't take the lead in that project. I really am not up to it. But using the cancer experience as an excuse feels like I am trying to worm my way out of something."

I asked her to find a way to frame it positively, and she flowed right into this wonderful, clear strong statement:

THIS IS WHERE I STAND

"I will say to them that I have had a lot of life experience, including being sick, and that has taught me what is really important in life, and what I can and can't do – and what I want and don't want to do – and I DON'T want to do this."

Standing up for herself.
Her knees felt fine!

15
HEALING YOUR
SENSITIVE
HEART

Sovereignty and the Spirit

It is probably clear to you by now that being sensitive is - can be - a wonderful gift.

And that it is misunderstood and misused by others, even by ourselves.

I believe that we are being asked from deep within ourselves to learn how to *be* sensitive and idealistic. To learn to nurture and maintain our strong sense of ourselves as individuals, while at the same time learning to find the oneness among us, with the world, and beyond.

I believe that we have been called by the earth itself, or by the being-ness of humanity, to take on this work. It doesn't really matter what church we belong to, or what our sense of spirituality is.

This is spiritual work at its deepest level, on behalf of humanity and the universe

We don't have any models for how to do this. Although there have probably always been idealistic sensitive people - the world would not have gotten so far along without them! – I think that it's possible that there are more of us now than ever before. And new humans are being born all the time who have new gifts and capacities. We are all stumbling along together in the dark, trying to figure out what works.

Our job continues to be to attempt to understand how to be who we are

As sensitive idealists, our job continues to be to attempt to understand how to be who we are, fully and deeply and profoundly and completely, and accept all that we are, even though we have all these *issues!!*

Here's a way
By doing this we're holding a space for those who come after us. I don't think of us canaries as being like sacrificial lambs, to mix my metaphors (taking full advantage of my artistic creative license as an HSP!), but rather as the way-showers.

Coming full circle
When she was about 19, I went with my younger daughter to a concert by Holly Near and Cris Williamson, two women

who have been standing strong and tall and out for the power of speaking your truth with your own voice on behalf of all of us for 30-plus years.

The concert was a wonderful, heartful experience to share with my daughter. It reflected some of my history and some of hers. She was 3 months old when she heard her first Cris Williamson concert in my lap!

Singing Stories

Two interesting images out of many: Holly sang and told a story about the empty place within us which is sometimes used by others to manipulate us into doing what they want us to do.

She sang about how that empty place is really the connection with the unknown… to be filled with the magic of our own creativity.

And how it reminds us that we don't ever know really what we are doing, and how important it is to honor those who have gone before us, because when we look back we can see what it was they were doing by what they left us. So it is important to keep doing what we can that is hopeful in each moment, so there will be something to see when our descendants look back.

Keep doing what is hopeful in each moment

The One, the many, the everyday

Holly also sang this wonderful a capella song about how the One is continually deciding to come to the earth as multitudes of individuals, to do things here that will make a difference, little and big things, famous and everyday things, living and dying with beauty, happy to know that we are all in this together.

Looking around and welcoming and greeting and thanking each other - saying "here we are."

So, you may be asking, this is all well and good, but if sensitive people are so special, how come so many of us are still so sick and tired???

One of our great wisdom teachers, Marion Woodman said: "When you are working with symptoms and trying to heal, the manifestation of the unconscious will come right through the body. As we are growing up, even in utero, all that is not bearable, we push down into the unconscious, into the body. The body carries the unconscious.

**All that is not bearable,
we push down into the unconscious,
into the body.
The body carries the unconscious**

"A trauma that we cannot allow ourselves to think about consciously is automatically pushed into the cells of the body, and the body carries it. This is the work of the therapist who works with someone and their rejected aspect....

"I try to create a safe space where we can go into meditation, go into the depths of the body, take the armoring off and let what is in the very depths come out. That's where the real energy and the real life are. That's where the 'I-am' is.

"I've seen people who could hardly walk because they were so burdened down with grief and depression – but once they contacted this, they were suddenly alive. They want to sing, they want to dance, they want to paint or make sculptures. Their whole creative life came alive...."

Quoted in *A Place at the Table*, by William Elliott

John's Story
This is an experience he had in a class I taught that I found very useful and powerful, myself, as an illustration of what we are talking about here. He did too.

John is a very thin, 55-year-old man who has had a chronic fatigue-like illness since age 19. In the last few years, as some of his symptoms have worsened, he has become mostly unemployed, and, at times, nearly paralysed with anxiety about his life and future.

He's an exquisitely creative writer, unpublished as of yet; a perfectionist (100 revisions!) who said once: "I am writing a book. I can't stop and publish it because who will I be when I am no longer writing a book??"

John appears quiet, but radiates a kind of hidden defiance, He has a lovely sweet spirit that often flashes out, a funny quick sense of humor. But his underlying sadness is apparent.

Being sensitive is a little bit shameful if you are a man. But being sensitive had advantages, so it was also a mixed thing.

I am sensitive to cold and air conditioning. Overhead lights. As a child I was extremely sensitive to having my feelings hurt. Even my skin was sensitive. My feelings were hurt very easily. I was angry a lot. My mother and father, they weren't trying to hurt me.

When you're a boy you attempt to cover up all that emotional stuff, try to not cry. If you are a boy crying, people make fun of you. Cruelty was common among boys, and I perpetuated it myself. Even girls were sometimes cruel.

If you're a **boy crying**, people make fun of you

It was a combination of mental, psychological and physical cruelty. For instance, I had a game where I'd suddenly change my personality to scare my younger sister. I was frustrated, so I took it out on others, constantly, and vice versa.

I miss me
There is this whole thing I concocted to get out of growing up. It has its drawbacks, but it works! Still, I miss being a

more powerful person. If I didn't have this illness and these fears, I would go more places, have more girlfriends, have more things that I wanted.

I have traded my power for safety

It's not quite that simple, but sort of. Most of the time I never felt that I was making decisions to be this way. Illness came along and knocked me over. There was not a damn thing I could do about it except to learn how to rest and go inward.

I think because I am male that I always pushed aside the notion of being sensitive. It is only recently that I can say I guess it is true. I'm still not sure about that.

There was not a damn thing I could do about it except to learn how to rest and go inward

In the early '70s there was a lot of stuff about sensitive men - they used their sensitivity to manipulate women. I feared that, because I disliked men who did it.

I was somebody who didn't pay attention to rest. Who thought about rest? I was 18.

I lost my youth, I lost the ability to establish a grounded, centered life based on having a job, and I lost possibilities. Lots of things I dreamed about doing became not possible to do.

The topic was sadness and depression
I opened the class by asking, "What breaks your heart?"

That was a prelude to asking, "What in your life, in your past, has broken your heart?"

The idea was that all heartbreaks are those too-painful-to-deal-with things that are stored in the body.

We discussed the concept, made lists and talked about what beliefs about ourselves and what's possible in the world would arise from heartbreak.

Then, in the midst of the EFT work we were doing to clear the trauma of the memories from the body, John suddenly said, "Can I interrupt?" I said sure, and he said,

"I just realized that I may not want to let go of this melancholy."

John had been coming to the class faithfully and attentively for several weeks, but in each class he said that he didn't get much effect from the EFT work we did. He'd done it a few times on his own and said it had helped "a little."

As we worked with his comment, he began to realize that feeling his melancholy made it possible for him to feel anything at all.

Eventually, as we talked about what hidden benefits this melancholy might have for his life, he said with a sheepish smile, "Well, I learned as a child that if you go around like a baby bird with your mouth open, people feed you..." Then he said, "If I let go of my melancholy, I might have to change my identity."

Feeling his melancholy made it possible for him to feel anything at all

"I might have to get a job, I might have to be successful, I might have to express my power, oh shit I might have to feel how angry I am. If I let go of all this *I don't know who I am.*"

"If I let go of my melancholy I might have to change my identity"

I was thinking that this shift in his perception of who he is in the world could be the opening for more of his true self to emerge.

Louisa, who read this story, asks:

Rue,

What is your thought on this: Why is an experience a trauma? What about the experience becomes traumatic for one person and what draws in this trauma to them and not another? I realize we are all individual, but some people seem prone to trauma after trauma in a lifetime and clearly others are not.

What about an experience becomes traumatic for one person, and what draws in this trauma to them and not another?

I think of the child, for example, who is tortured or deeply traumatized by an external predator and the family is in shock.

Is this also his personal unconscious at work - perhaps a hidden belief??? How can we better understand and heal such matters, I wonder?

Louisa

I love this evocative question about why is an experience a trauma!! It is exactly the kind of "first cause" question that I always find coming to my mind.

My favorite answer to this question has its origin in TCM,

Profoundly light-hearted strategies for unsticking stuck stuff

Traditional Chinese Medicine. In the TCM model, the Heart is the body's most intelligent system. It puts out 50-60 times more electrical charge than the brain does (I'm capitalizing the Heart because it is seen in this tradition as more than just the physical organ). In TCM thinking, the Heart houses the body's spirit.

The Heart is the body's most intelligent system

When we perceive a negative experience, a disharmony is created in the body's energy system, and a misalignment occurs in the body-mind-spirit.

The lyrical part of this model, for me, is in the description of how we form at conception, and how the patterns are formed that become the blueprint for how we experience the world, all of our bugaboos. Maybe that is another way of describing the lensing system for the soul that we think of as the personality.

TCM says that in the forming fetus, the first beat of the heart gives us our human identity, and sets off a cascade of quickening

At the next heartbeat the amygdala, an organ in the brain's limbic system, what we call the reptilian brain, begins to form.

The amygdala's job is to record, store, and be on the alert for danger signs. It sends signals to the brain and body that are interpreted as fear, leading to what we know as the "fight, flight or freeze" response.

Patterns from before birth

As the amygdala forms, it records the energetic patterns of all the mother's emotional responses to her memories, experiences, thought patterns - not only all of her joys but specifically all that she fears, all the triggers that make her anxious, upset, angry, worried. I'm wondering if the same coding must be in the DNA of the father's sperm as well, adding his "stuff" to the mix.

The amygdala continues to record the mother's emotional experience for the whole time of the pregnancy. It works steadily, recording all the dangers we must watch out for, up until we reach the age of three or so when the conscious mind begins to activate.

These energetic patterns lie in our unconscious, recorded in our very physiology at the cellular level, awaiting awakening by our own life experiences.

Family patterns

In effect, they are the codings for the belief systems - whether constricted, obstructed or not - that form our family belief culture handed down through the generations.

I personally think they are coded triggers for fear, anger and sadness, so that our experiences, particularly as children, awaken in us what we *think* we should react to, and we react automatically.

Profoundly light-hearted strategies for unsticking stuck stuff

The limbic system works below the level of conscious thought

So even though we "know" our reaction "doesn't make sense," we can't stop it by thinking or talking about it because it happens at the unconscious level, flashing into a body response before the mind gets engaged.

I think that what we call trauma is our deep, soul level response to whatever constricts or misaligns the flow of spirit, the emergent, creative, generative flow of spirit through us

A traumatic experience seems to be anything that makes us feel disconnected from our birthright as a human, the conscious physical experience of:

※ *Belonging*
※ *Being visible*
※ *Being heard*
※ *Feeling safe, worthy, heard, deserving*
※ *Expressing our own truth*

Those old ancestral family beliefs are usually about personal and global hopelessness, helplessness and worthlessness, and having to take care of others - Save the World! - before you can take care of yourself.

Of course we never get to taking care of self – there are always so many others who come first!

We never feel we have the right to make life choices that lead to *us* feeling good. Traditional Christianity always warns us against being "selfish." I like to reframe the word "selfish" as SELF-ish: that is, anything that is care for the soul.

Trauma is the suffering of our deepest self in response to a feeling of the loss of our sense of sovereignty

The amygdala is hardwired, so to speak, to continue its valiant efforts to protect us from danger, to be hypervigilant, racing in front, trying to keep us safe from whatever we fear is out there, so that when we get there we will be all right.

But really it just reinforces our feeling of being a victim, always at risk. All those experiences of being rejected and hurt are continual evidence that we were right in our assessment that the world is a dangerous and scary place.

We tend to either retreat, or come out swinging or, more likely for a sensitive person, we *freeze*, held in place by fear. If we freeze long enough, the body evolves this into chronic pain or illness.

Continuing John's Story...

I believe that the pain in John's body is the physical manifestation of mental, emotional, and spiritual pain that he has not been able to deal with or look at, so he has pushed it down, stuffed it into his body.

Eventually stuffed emotions emerge as physical pain and dis-ease

His melancholy, is, I think, a protective layer he has built around himself that justifies his being powerless and taken care of because he doesn't know how to act from his deep sovereignty. So his insight that if he releases his melancholy he will have to change his identity is true, and very scary to him.

EFT and other energy psychology techniques

These techniques work with the energetic patterns in the brain and the body to "uncouple" negative emotion from the experiences that generated the beliefs and the feelings of suffering. I teach people these techniques so they can do this work for themselves, not just come to me to "be fixed."

There is ample research now showing that when a person's belief system about himself and how to be in the world changes, the brain itself actually changes. It follows that one's experience of the world then changes.

Belief change = experiential shift

Energy psychology work can help to restore alignment with spirit. It can restore the capacity to choose more satisfying and fulfilling options, and one's response to life and experiences, rather than being stuck, reacting in the same old painful, unproductive ways we have gotten used to and that we thought we were the victim of.

Veterans

Energy psychology work has been done with profound effectiveness with veterans who experience PTSD. After being treated, they were able to recall the terrible things they were asked to do and that they experienced in wartime, without re-experiencing the trauma in their minds, bodies, emotions and spirits. The memories are still there, but they have lost their initial, horrific charge, their meaning.

The meaning is the key

The traumatic experience is still there in the person's mind, but it no longer means what it used to mean when those unconscious belief systems got triggered by the experiences.

The importance lies within the meaning that a person makes about an experience, what it apparently means *about* him or her and life in this world – there lies the suffering and the pain. And that meaning can be changed.

The only true healing, then, is healing the Heart

So, back to the TCM model of the body's spirit housed in the Heart: the only true healing, then, is healing of the heart in the deepest, broadest, most universal sense.

In an individual, that means healing any unconscious belief patterns that we have inherited genetically that constrict our ability to love ourselves and honor our sovereignty.

NOTES

Profoundly light-hearted strategies for unsticking stuck stuff

16
SOVEREIGNTY

What is it?

Applying it to our own lives
I have used the word "sovereignty" a few times, and I want to take a minute to explain what I mean by it.

We think of sovereignty as having to do with kingship, or in the sense of a "sovereign nation."

We don't usually apply the word
sovereignty
to ourselves.

Why not?

Who am I within this relationship?
I worked with a woman who was suffering from a failed relationship. When I asked her if she could define the moment she realized that it was not going to work, she instantly said yes.

She described an intimate moment that she called "Falling

into Darkness." She had felt herself totally open to this man. In that moment she became aware of his fear of deep connection, his withdrawal away from their shared connection, away from her, back into himself.

Opening
She had opened to him from her sensitive nature, connecting with the deep part of him, wanting to create and hold a space that was big enough and strong enough that he could feel safe enough to respond to that place in her. When he wasn't able to move past his own fear, he withdrew.

Abandonment
She interpreted this as "I am not enough. There must be something wrong with me." It brought up all her feelings of abandonment from experiences in her past. She perceived "all" those people who had left her - either innocently, or because of their own insecurities and fears.

There must be something wrong with me!

But is there, really?

We often interpret those situations as "there is something wrong with me." And we fall into despair once again. How often do we do this very thing to ourselves in a given day? I know from experience it doesn't take much! The slightest hint of criticism, of being left or left out, of a connection breaking, even briefly, even when logically I know it isn't...

THIS IS WHERE I STAND

There is that lovely e.e. cummings poem:

somewhere i have never travelled, gladly beyond
any experience, your eyes have their silence:
in your most frail gesture are things which enclose me,
or which i cannot touch because they are too near

your slightest look easily will unclose me
though i have closed myself as fingers,
you open always petal by petal myself as Spring opens
(touching skillfully, mysteriously) her first rose

or if your wish be to close me, i and
my life will shut very beautifully, suddenly,
as when the heart of this flower imagines
the snow carefully everywhere descending;

nothing which we are to perceive in this world equals
the power of your intense fragility: whose texture
compels me with the colour of its countries,
rendering death and forever with each breathing

(i do not know what it is about you that closes
and opens; only something in me understands
the voice of your eyes is deeper than all roses)
nobody, not even the rain, has such small hands

e.e.cummings

(Permission to reprint pending)

Profoundly light-hearted strategies for unsticking stuck stuff

See me!

Don't we wish that someone could see us this deeply? And when they predictably don't, we fall into darkness. And we make it about us, something wrong with us. It is "my inadequacy, my unworthiness."

Noticing The Moment

One of my clients and I worked with finding the inner signal in her body that was letting her know that she was about to "leave." She said she would begin to feel blank.

We tapped for choosing in that moment of going blank to "stay in me, and remember how freeing that feels." As we tapped, she remembered a powerful time when she had experienced being under emotional siege, and instead of "leaving," she stayed. We brought that empowering incident into her EFT Choice statement.

When we normally feel like "leaving" we can now choose to stay!

The queen

When I think about unworthiness, sometimes I think of my mother.

I woke up in the middle of the night one night, trying to think of a way to describe my mother for her home health care coordinator who I thought was not quite getting who she was.

Profoundly light-hearted strategies for unsticking stuck stuff

My mother is in her late 80s, an extremely sensitive person, especially to any possible slights. I was finding it hard to explain how my mother is: more than the fuzzy-minded, sometimes sweet person, but often seeming to be a stubborn and cranky old lady.

The image came to me of a Queen - without a crown. I began thinking of other images that had the same sense of strong Presence, but Presence hidden, made invisible or obstructed. Perhaps... an opera singer without a voice, or maybe a wizard without a staff - somehow the sense of the very intention of the incarnation having only a blocked channel to flow through.

The thwarted queen

My mother has the aspect to me of someone who has great power, awareness and wisdom, and a gracious heart, but who has seldom been able to exercise these capacities, or known how to use them, or even had the assurance that they were there at all. She was dominated in her growing up years by two older brothers whom she, and obviously her parents, idolized and favored.

Her life has reflected the pattern of, "No one ever lets me speak!" Over the years her power has constricted itself into passive aggressive criticism, narcissism and a victim mentality.

It suddenly occurred to me that I was thinking about obstructed sovereignty.

Pure ME

Somehow, *way* behind our sense of unworthiness, and obscured from view, especially our own, I believe there is actually a pure sense of one's own perfection and radiant beauty. The sacred.

(Now - a brief word to the wise - fit what I am saying into your own spiritual context. I am not trying to proselytize here for any religion or way of thinking.)

I suspect that all our (often unconscious) beliefs, actions, positioning, and emotions are simply distortions, smoke-screens, to obscure the knowledge of our own sacred sovereignty, even - or maybe especially - from ourselves. We do this for all kinds of reasons, I think, but they all add up to not feeling able to safely be who we really are in the world.

Fatal protection

I believe that all the energy that goes into maintaining the contortions that keep our feeling of unworthiness in place has the positive intention of protecting us, perhaps even to the point of killing us.

My "falling into darkness" client said, "My despair has sometimes come up as a death wish." When I asked her what would be the benefits of dying, she said, "I would be free from the struggle of living."

I CAN be free of this struggle

She recognized that she had been "going out of herself" (as sensitive people, we are REALLY good at this) to "be in" her partner, so she could know what he needed, and then try to be that for him. Our session focused on empowering the

Profoundly light-hearted strategies for unsticking stuck stuff

choice to stay in herself, and to recognize how freeing and safe that really, in truth, was.

I have worked with so many sensitive people who, when they looked deeply into a limiting belief or behavior, found an unconscious intention to secure peace, safety, beauty, lightness, love - "heaven," in other words.

But the part of them that was trying to attain all that had very ineffective strategies, probably put in place long ago, and most certainly picked up from family belief patterns on the way into their incarnation.

Emotions are messengers!

These self-same strategies are, in fact, no longer appropriate for the person we are right now, and can most likely even be damaging. Those protective parts just keep on running the same old patterns with the same old desperation, and getting the same old results without realizing it. Tunnel vision.

This always makes me think of the woman who was devastated when she had a stroke and didn't die - and assumed that "even God didn't think she was good enough," and therefore rejected her.

I believe that ALL of our "negative emotions" are messengers about our true worth. If it were actually true that we were unworthy, we wouldn't be so sad, mad, scared.

The devastation she felt was telling - it said that a very important part of her felt unbearably wounded by the very thought that even God didn't think she was good enough. That meant to me that there was an essential beingness in

Profoundly light-hearted strategies for unsticking stuck stuff

her that DID NOT BELIEVE THIS THOUGHT AND KNEW SHE WAS WORTH WAY MORE THAN THAT. Sorry for shouting! Important point!

So I believe that any "therapy" that reveals our sovereignty - our essential sacred beingness - to ourselves, so we can be and function in the world in our own inimitable way - would be a good thing.

David Spangler

One of my most favorite philosopher-spiritual teacher-wise persons is David Spangler. He is also a father of four and a really nice person who has a regular life in the world. That counts for a lot to me – it says that he has a lot of practice in applying his inner awareness to being a real person in the real world. You might be interested in checking out his organization's website at lorian.org.

True Name
David talks about sovereignty, using the term "true name."

A true name puts me in touch with the power to connect and engage with life in a creative fashion. But when I name myself unworthy, I am actually disconnecting and diminishing my capacity to engage creatively. I am doing the opposite of what a true name does.

Unworthiness is a punishing name, not an empowering name. It may sound descriptive but it is not. It is a judgment upon myself, not a description of who I am. Unworthiness may have power over my thinking, but it is not a name of power.

The world knows our True Names

A true name may be thought of as something that is private and secret, and in the arena of ordinary human interaction this is correct. But the world knows our true names. That is the point. Our true names are how we are known to spirit and to the creative powers of life within the world. They are our names of participation in the community of life and the co-creative unfolding of the world.

In the Light Space
I once had an experience about this.

I was sitting on my lawn near a row of fir trees when a voice popped into my mind. It said, "the trees know your true name." This was surprising as I had not been thinking about true names at all, nor for that matter of the trees. The voice continued. "Just sit and let the trees remind you who you are. Let them speak your name."

Then I had a vision.

Just sit and let the trees remind you who you are

I saw myself in an in-between place, a liminal state between the domain where I dwell as soul and this physical world. I had not yet been born. I was in a kind of "anteroom" to the material world and to physical incarnation. At first, this place didn't look like anything at all, just an expanse of white light, rather like the "loading program" in the movie, *The Matrix*, when Morpheus is first introducing Neo to the "real world."

As I watched, I saw myself in a clearing near a forest. Out from the forest came numerous different animals, birds, insects...the creatures of the earth. All of them, including the trees in the forest itself and the stones in the soil and other plants, were witnessing me... I have no other word for it... they were learning my "name." Not the sounds "David Spangler," but the name formed by my intent as a soul for this incarnation.

And they were adding to that name. In this sense, it was like a gifting ceremony one reads about in fairy tales, where animals and spiritual beings like faeries gather to bless and give gifts to a newborn. And in so doing, they were both welcoming me and weaving me into the fabric of the world into which I was being born.

MY Name, the name formed by my intent as a soul for this incarnation

In this way, my inner name was being fashioned from my intent as a soul but also from the intents and qualities of the world soul itself and the fellow creatures into whose circle of life I was about to enter.

It was very clear in this vision that this process was symbolic of a welcoming, a weaving, and a "naming" that goes on for every soul that incarnates into this world.

A welcoming, a weaving, and a "naming"

After this vision, I realized that the natural things around me, particularly in my case the stones and trees, for which I have always felt an affinity, knew me in ways I did not always know myself. They knew me in a deep way, an incarnational way, an ancient way. They knew my "true name."

I found that by sitting with them and just sharing presence with them, being open to their witnessing of me, took me into an inner place where I could touch my true name myself, no matter what other human or emotional names I might call myself from time to time.

Though I might name myself "failure," or "unworthy," they never do, but always bear witness to the deeper name of my connectedness to earth and life.

Connecting

David offers the following exercise, created from his own experience:
This exercise is simple, but can be a very powerful experience.

Part I
Go out into nature.
It could be as close as your front or back yard (you don't have to climb the Tetons or go to Yosemite for this one!); for

Profoundly light-hearted strategies for unsticking stuck stuff

that matter, you can do this exercise with a plant or a stone you may have in your house.

Enter into stillness and silence for a moment.
Doing so gives your energy a chance to settle down, your attention to become relaxed and centered, and your mind and heart ready for something new.

Now stand or sit in front of a tree or stone or some natural object, and allow yourself to be seen by it.
How do you appear to this presence?
How do you think it sees you?
What is it like to be seen by a tree, a stone, or by nature itself?

Part II

Repeat Part I -
This time remember that this presence before you that is seeing you is part of the world that welcomed you, saw you, and participated in your Naming. As you are seen by it, let it remind you of who you are. Let it remind you of your True Name.

Another idea....
If you choose to do this exercise, and some part of it doesn't make sense or is incongruent for you, just find your own way to do it. What you create for yourself is way more important than following someone else's directions!

Rue
A bit of background about me here: I grew up feeling like my parents were raising this girl "over there," (imagine me

gesturing over to the side). She was out of some book that had all the rules about how a girl was supposed to be.

My parents were good people, and I am appreciative of all that they provided for me. But I was this completely *other* girl over *here*. I never felt that they actually saw who I was. Consequently, I grew up feeling invisible, not present, unseen.

When I first did David's exercise I began to have a cascade of reframing - new ideas, new contexts - around the word "invisible."

In addition to loving the connection with the earth that it opened in me, I began to get a sense of my True Name as actually BEING "Invisible" - but in the sense of in-visible - "seeing within," inwardly visioning.

I have a Gift for Seeing
WE have a Gift for Seeing!

As a Sensitive Idealist I do have an ability, a gift, for seeing a truth within its outer appearance. This truth is often camouflaged by a person's exterior behavior or words, or within a flow of events. So I am aware of that person's Truth not as a vision, in the mystical sense, but in an ongoing grounded present-moment sense of Presence - a sense of this person's unique flow of Truth within the flow of life.

I think actually that I have developed this gift out of the pain and challenge of feeling invisible, unseen as a child and young adult. So, it follows that the idea that our True Name grows with us, even generates and fosters growth.

My True Name
My sense of my True Name has a quality of Truth Seer / Truth Sayer.

I had a funny flash of the word, "T-Rue." As I did the exercise, I had the strongest sense of being Seen by animals and trees and sunshine and water.

What a wonderful and life changing experience this was for me! And can be for you....

The following poem speaks to me of all of this:

Invisible Work

Because no one could ever praise me enough,
because I don't mean these poems only
but the unseen
unbelievable effort it takes to live
the life that goes on between them,
I think all the time about invisible work.
About the young mother on Welfare
I interviewed years ago,
who said, "It's hard.

THIS IS WHERE I STAND

You bring him to the park,
run rings around yourself keeping him safe,
cut hot dogs into bite-sized pieces for dinner,
and there's no one
to say what a good job you're doing,
how you were patient and loving
for the thousandth time even though you had a headache."

And I, who am used to feeling sorry for myself
because I am lonely,
when all the while,
as the Chippewa poem says,
I am being carried
by great winds across the sky,
thought of the invisible work that stitches up the world day
and night,
the slow, unglamorous work of healing,
the way worms in the garden
tunnel ceaselessly so the earth can breathe
and bees ransack this world into being,
while owls and poets stalk shadows,
our loneliest labors under the moon.

There are mothers
for everything, and the sea
is a mother too,
whispering and whispering to us
long after we have stopped listening.

Profoundly light-hearted strategies for unsticking stuck stuff

I stopped and let myself lean
a moment, against the blue
shoulder of the air. The work
of my heart
is the work of the world's heart.

There is no other art.

Alison Luterman

**The work
of my heart
is the work of the
world's
heart**

**There is
no other
art**

17
MANAGE YOUR EXPERIENCE

A few more techniques

As a sensitive person, I have found these tools useful for managing my experience in the world

Pull in Your Energy Field

This first one I learned in a moment of challenge, although it probably has roots in some ancient spiritual technique.

When my younger daughter was about 9, she and I and her father went to a sort of rummage sale held by the university's athletic department to get rid of their excess equipment. There was a huge crowd – all the jocks in town must have been there!

We were squeezed into a small space, waiting for them to open the doors to all the treasures. When the door finally opened there was a massive crush of large people moving forward.

I was having a hard time breathing and feeling incredibly claustrophobic.

I looked over at my daughter and realized that she, being maybe the smallest person there (*and* extremely sensitive), was on the verge of panic. We were stuck in place, couldn't move, hard to breathe, and it felt scary dangerous.

Lickety split ingenuity!
Inventing quickly on the spot, I said, "Pull in your aura! Pull in your energy field, all the way inside you! Breathe slooooowly and deeply."

I don't know what she thought I meant by that – I hardly knew what I meant myself – but she did whatever she did, and I did too, and we both made it through the door safely and began sidling toward the edge of the crowd into an open space.

Whatever we both did worked, and I have been using that technique ever since. Especially when I am in a crowd, or shopping in an intense place, like WalMart, for instance. Or in a context where the energy level or the noise level feels uncomfortable or threatening.

My personal Egg of Safety
* I pull in my energy field from all sides, top and bottom too, feeling that happen (or imagining it).

* I imagine that I am placing my energy field into a crystal box somewhere near my heart.

＊ From that center, I imagine that I am pulsing out a sphere of energy that takes an egg shape around me.

＊ I fill it with light, sometimes white, blue, lavender, whatever feels right at the time.

＊ I imagine that the outer edge of this sphere is made of material that repulses any energy that will not benefit my well-being, and yet it will allow in anything that is good for me.

I used this technique a lot with both my daughters as they were growing up. Though they are in their twenties now, and live elsewhere with their own lives, still, when we are together in an uncomfortable or overwhelming situation, one of them is sure to say, "Mom! Remember to pull your aura in!" I smile on the inside.

The Cleansing Whirlwind of White Light

My husband Timothy learned this technique when he was studying the work of the Rainbow Bridge.

I find it useful when I feel that my energy field has maybe picked up too much of someone's negative energy, or the scattered, un-integrated energy of a place.

＊ Imagine that over your head, about 12 inches up, is a powerful source of white light.

＊ Let it swirl in a whirlwind down through your body, extending it out beyond your skin for several inches.

✳ Swirl the whirlwind all the way deep down into the earth. Do this for as long as you like.

✳ Then with your breath, imagine that you are pulling earthlight up from the center of the earth into your body, circulating around your heart, and out through the top of your head.

(adapted from a technique described in The Rainbow Bridge, RainbowBridge Productions, Box 929, Danville, California 94526)

Smile Down into your Body

A lovely, brief, and very effective technique for giving yourself a radiant feeling.

This is an old Taoist technique for becoming Well and Rested.

✳ Imagine that you are smiling down inside your body.

✳ Send a smile into all your organs, or into a place in your body that particularly needs it.

Just smile into your body!

✳ Imagine that you are sitting or standing in a smile. The smile of the sun, God's smile, whatever works for you.

More
For many more protective, clearing and healing techniques

I recommend *Energy Medicine,* by Donna Eden, and *Psychic Protection: Creating Positive Energies For People And Places* by William Bloom.

Focusing on and Creating exactly what **we** want

At a conference recently, I had the wonderful opportunity to dine with Carol Look, another EFT pro I admire immensely (CarolLook.com).

Carol specializes in anxiety relief, abundance and weight loss. I noticed that she ate her food with such gusto and appreciation, and had dessert with each meal. Finally I asked her how she managed to eat so much and stay thin. I loved her answer so much that I am using it to reframe all kinds of things in my life. She said:

"I welcome thin-ness, instead of pushing away weight gain."

What a wonderful thought! In our diligent search to find and correct everything wrong with us (or misuse our energy by creating red-herrings like illness or weight or _____ to distract us and others from noticing that we are really just "selfishly" doing what we want to do), it maybe hadn't occurred to us that we are, in doing that: actually misusing our energy!

Instead of thinking of our sensitivity as a fault, a not-enough-ness, and pushing it away, let us welcome it!

NOTES

Profoundly light-hearted strategies for unsticking stuck stuff

18
HEALING THE HEART OF THE WORLD

A Good Question

When I first made up "The World is My Oracle" technique, I asked myself this question:
"What makes us frame our experience negatively?"

✳ Then, I told the Universe that for the next 20 minutes I would pay close attention to what caught my awareness.

✳ I held that intention on the drive home in my car.

✳ Right away on the way home I saw a billboard that said "Overworking your heart?"

✳ Then I saw a bumper sticker that said, "If you praise your kids they will bloom." (The reverse implication being, of course, that if you don't praise your kids, they will wilt!)

✳ And then I went by a movie theater with a double feature that ran two titles together looking like one, a most evocative thought: "IMAGINARY HEROES BORN IN A BROTHEL"

I laughed as I flashed on these thoughts:

Here we are, highly sensitive, bold, bright, beautiful sovereign beings from the imaginal realm, coming to be the shining heroes of our own story and that of the planet, and then - yikes! - we're born into a bewildering environment of distorted concepts of love, power and purpose!

Doing our best, battling our inner demons with faith and courage…overworking our hearts, believing that we are not up to the desperate task of protecting our spirit in an unsafe unfriendly universe - and poor us, never having gotten enough praise ourselves from parents who never got enough praise because our grandparents never got enough praise, we wilt.

On the whole, the world doesn't know yet that the very universe blooms when any of us smiles.

Well, hey, thanks universe, I thought to myself. Very interesting answer!

Sweets at the end
I had just written those words, and was thinking – so is this the end of the book? I wanted some nice, positive story to end with. I went looking for an email that I remembered from a telephone client, definitely a highly sensitive idealist type, in which she had talked about her healing process.

Profoundly light-hearted strategies for unsticking stuck stuff

She praised EFT, and spoke positively about her long road out of the painful and traumatic effects of a very difficult childhood, and also spoke positively about herself.

It is only recently that she has been able to say good things about herself. Now often her words are even radiantly appreciative when she talks about her progress. She is SO grateful to have learned EFT.

I couldn't find the email, even though I have all of our correspondence in a folder - somewhere. But I happened across an email from someone else from six months ago, and for some reason I missed it at the time and it hadn't gotten deleted.

Reading this message now, I thought, "Well, the world is at it again!" This story brought a lump to my throat and tears to my eyes. It is a wonderful metaphor for finishing our conversation on healing – healing ourselves, healing each other, healing the world. Just by being the best of who we are, in the moment that we are in, now.

On the following pages is a story that reinforces my firm belief that love is exactly what Longfellow so eloquently wrote :

The thread
of all sustaining beauty
that runs through all and
doth all unite

Profoundly light-hearted strategies for unsticking stuck stuff

The Hawaiian island of Maui has been called the heart chakra of the planet, and for good reason - it's the perfect blending of land and ocean. Both humans and mammals know it and feed off it.

Jennifer Anderson, a charter boat dive leader in Maui, describes her magic breathtaking moment in the ocean off Maui with a wounded giant 15-foot Manta ray. This article will touch my heart forever.

This Magic Moment
by Jennifer Anderson

It was like many Maui mornings, the sun rising over Haleakala as we greeted our divers for the day's charter. As my captain and I explained the dive procedures, I noticed the wind line moving into Molokini, a small, crescent-shaped island that harbors a large reef.

I slid through the briefing, then prompted my divers to gear up, careful to do everything right so the divers would feel confident with me, the dive leader.

The dive went pretty close to how I had described it: The garden eels performed their underwater ballet, the parrot fish grazed on the coral, and the ever-elusive male flame wrasse flared their colors to defend their territory.

Near the last level of the dive, two couples in my group signaled they were going to ascend. As luck would have it, the remaining divers were two European brothers, who were obviously troubled by the idea of a "woman" dive master and had ignored me for the entire dive.

Profoundly light-hearted strategies for unsticking stuck stuff

THIS IS WHERE I STAND

The three of us caught the current and drifted along the outside of the reef, slowly beginning our ascent until, far below, something caught my eye. After a few moments, I made out the white shoulder patches of a manta ray in about one hundred and twenty feet of water.

Manta rays are one of my greatest loves, but very little is known about them. They feed on plankton, which makes them more delicate than an aquarium can handle. They travel the oceans wide - they're a complete mystery.

Mantas can be identified by the distinctive pattern on their belly, with no two rays alike. In 1992, I had been identifying the manta rays that were seen at Molokini and found that some were known, but many more were sighted only once, and then gone.

So there I was... a beautiful, very large ray beneath me and my skeptical divers behind. I reminded myself that I was still trying to win their confidence, and a bounce to see this manta wouldn't help my case.

So I started calling through my regulator, "Hey, come up and see me!" I had tried this before to attract the attention of whales and dolphins, who are very chatty underwater and will come sometimes just to see what the noise is about. My divers were just as puzzled by my actions, but continued to try to ignore me.

There was another dive group ahead of us. The leader, who was a friend of mine and knew me to be fairly sane, stopped to see what I was doing. I kept calling to the ray, and when

Profoundly light-hearted strategies for unsticking stuck stuff

she shifted in the water column, I took that as a sign that she was curious. So I started waving my arms, calling her up to me.

After a minute, she lifted away from where she had been riding the current and began to make a wide circular glide until she was closer to me. I kept watching as she slowly moved back and forth, rising higher, until she was directly beneath the two Europeans and me. I looked at them and was pleased to see them smiling. Now they liked me. After all, I could call up a manta ray!

Looking back to the ray, I realized she was much bigger than what we were used to around Molokini - a good fifteen feet from wing tip to wing tip, and not a familiar-looking ray. I had not seen this animal before. There was something else odd about her. I just couldn't figure out what it was.

Once my brain clicked in and I was able to concentrate, I saw deep V-shaped marks of her flesh missing from her backside. Other marks ran up and down her body. At first I thought a boat had hit her. As she came closer, now with only ten feet separating us, I realized what was wrong.

She had fishing hooks embedded in her head by her eye, with very thick fishing line running to her tail. She had rolled with the line and was wrapped head to tail about five or six times. The line had torn into her body at the back, and those were the V-shaped chunks that were missing.

I felt sick and, for a moment, paralyzed. I knew wild animals in pain would never tolerate a human to inflict more pain. But I had to do something.

THIS IS WHERE I STAND

Forgetting about my air, my divers and where I was, I went to the manta. I moved very slowly and talked to her the whole time, like she was one of the horses I had grown up with. When I touched her, her whole body quivered, like my horse would. I put both of my hands on her, then my entire body, talking to her the whole time. I knew that she could knock me off at any time with one flick of her great wing.

When she had steadied, I took out the knife that I carry on my inflator hose and lifted one of the lines. It was tight and difficult to get my finger under, almost like a guitar string. She shook, which told me to be gentle. It was obvious that the slightest pressure was painful.

As I cut through the first line, it pulled into her wounds. With one beat of her mighty wings, she dumped me and bolted away. I figured that she was gone and was amazed when she turned and came right back to me, gliding under my body. I went to work.

She seemed to know it would hurt, and somehow, she also knew that I could help. Imagine the intelligence of that creature, to come for help and to trust!

I cut through one line and into the next until she had all she could take of me and would move away, only to return in a moment or two. I never chased her. I would never chase any animal. I never grabbed her. I allowed her to be in charge, and she always came back.

When all the lines were cut on top, on her next pass, I went under her to pull the lines through the wounds at the back of her body. The tissue had started to grow around them, and they were difficult to get loose. I held myself against her body, with my hand on her lower jaw. She held as motionless as she could.

When it was all loose, I let her go and watched her swim in a circle. She could have gone then, and it would have all fallen away. She came back, and I went back on top of her.

The fishing hooks were still in her. One was barely hanging on, which I removed easily. The other was buried by her eye at least two inches past the barb. Carefully, I began to take it out, hoping I wasn't damaging anything. She did open and close her eye while I worked on her, and finally, it was out. I held the hooks in one hand, while I gathered the fishing line in the other hand, my weight on the manta.

I could have stayed there forever! I was totally oblivious to everything but that moment. I loved this manta. I was so moved that she would allow me to do this to her. But reality came screaming down on me. With my air running out, I reluctantly came to my senses and pushed myself away.

At first, she stayed below me. And then, when she realized that she was free, she came to life like I never would have imagined she could. I thought she was sick and weak, since her mouth had been tied closed, and she hadn't been able to feed for however long the lines had been on her. I thought wrong! With two beats of those powerful wings, she rocketed along the wall of Molokini and then directly out to sea!

I lost view of her and, remembering my divers, turned to look for them. Remarkably, we hadn't traveled very far. My divers were right above me and had witnessed the whole event, thankfully! No one would have believed me alone. It seemed too amazing to have really happened.

But as I looked at the hooks and line in my hands and felt the torn calluses from her rough skin, I knew that, yes, it really had happened.

I kicked in the direction of my divers, whose eyes were still wide from the encounter, only to have them signal me to stop and turn around. Until this moment, the whole experience had been phenomenal, but I could explain it.

Now, the moment turned magical. I turned and saw her slowly gliding toward me. With barely an effort, she approached me and stopped, her wing just touching my head. I looked into her round, dark eye, and she looked deeply into me.

I felt a rush of something that so overpowered me I have yet to find the words to describe it, except a warm and loving flow of energy from her into me. She stayed with me for a moment. I don't know if it was a second or an hour. Then, as sweetly as she came back, she lifted her wing over my head and was gone. A manta thank-you.

I hung in midwater, using the safety-stop excuse, and tried to make sense of what I had experienced. Eventually, collecting myself, I surfaced and was greeted by an ecstatic group of divers and a curious captain. They all gave me time to get my heart started and to begin to breathe.

Sadly, I have not seen her since that day, and I am still looking. For the longest time, though my wetsuit was tattered

Profoundly light-hearted strategies for unsticking stuck stuff

and torn, I would not change it because I thought she wouldn't recognize me. I call to every manta I see, and they almost always acknowledge me in some way.

One day, though, it will be her. She'll hear me and pause, remembering the giant cleaner that she trusted to relieve her pain, and she'll come. At least that is how it happens in my dreams.

(Generous permission to use article granted by Jennifer Anderson)

On the Road to Well and Rested

The word trauma means "wound."

It is only in the last 115 years or so that "trauma" has been used in the sense of psychic wound.

Psychic wound – a wounding of the soul. In healing the wounds of our beliefs about our sensitivity, we heal our souls, we heal the soul of the earth.

What a blessing we have in EFT, and the other Energy Psychology techniques. In the use of this blessing for ourselves and others, we can touch the space in each of us where we become a blessing, just by being. No expectations to meet, nothing we have to do to become worthy.

In healing the wounds of our beliefs about our sensitivity, we heal our souls, we heal the soul of the earth

I believe that each of us is called to the earth, by the earth itself, to offer the blessing of our personal transformation. I have heard so many people lament that their lives have been wasted, trying in vain to deal with all the pain.

It's the Journey that counts

I truly believe that what is asked of us *is* our actual healing process. It is not that we "get healed" and then we go out into the world to "save it" or do "good works."

It is our very healing process itself that is the blessing

All we have to do is intend it. When we *live the questions,* as the German poet Rilke said, rather than struggle to find answers, we find ourselves living into the answers. And there, in that flow, lies the healing.

Every one of our moments counts - Be your best you in each moment

Wild Geese
by Mary Oliver

You do not have to be good.
You do not have to walk on your knees
for a hundred miles through the desert repenting.
You only have to let the soft animal of your body
love what it loves.

Tell me about despair, yours, and I will tell you mine.
Meanwhile the world goes on.
Meanwhile the sun and the clear pebbles of the rain
are moving across the landscapes,
over the prairies and the deep trees,
the mountains and the rivers.

Meanwhile the wild geese, high in the clean blue air,
are heading home again.

Whoever you are, no matter how lonely,
the world offers itself to your imagination,
calls to you like the wild geese, harsh and exciting—
over and over announcing your place
        in the family of things.

(Printed with permission: see page 206)

19
STAND STRONG & SENSITIVE WITH EFT

The Emotional Freedom Techniques!

Any kind of chronic pain - whether physical, emotional or mental - is about what we believe about our experience.

Limiting beliefs create a disruption in the body's energy field. Learn and use EFT to neutralize these limiting beliefs (see ch. 11 for EFT instructions). Starting with the Karate Chop point or the Sore Spot, use the following EFT setups.

Even though ...
> I worry that I am TOO sensitive
> I feel so deeply
> I am so open to others' emotions
> I am easily hurt and upset
> I don't like conflict
> It's hard to stop feeling sad sometimes
> I can't watch the news or sad or violent movies
> I get depressed easily
> I get overwhelmed

I deeply and completely love and accept myself

Even though ...

     I can't stand large crowds

     I can't take loud noise

     I don't like hectic environments

     I wish I were tougher and could let things roll off easier

     I think my sensitivity is a weakness

     I think something is wrong with me. It is my fault.

     I wish things didn't bother me so much

     I wish my emotions weren't so obvious to other people

     I wish I could let things go and not worry so much

     I hide my sensitivity from others

I deeply and completely love and accept myself

Now Break out of
The Cage of the P.A.S.S.T.

1. What have people said to you about your sensitivity?

> *Tap on:*
> *Even though people have said _____ ,*
> *I deeply and completely love and accept myself*

2. How has that made you feel??
Where do you feel it in your body?

> *Tap on the feelings and emotion in your body*

Profoundly light-hearted strategies for unsticking stuck stuff

3. What did you come to believe about yourself as a result?

> *Tap on the beliefs*

4. Choose a specific disturbing incident from your life connected with being sensitive.

> *Make a movie or inner story of the specific incident.*
> *Give it a title.*
> *Note details: clear, fuzzy, movement, still, sound, silent, etc.*

> NOW TAP:

> *Tap on the title:*
> *Even though I have this (title) _____ story in my body about being sensitive...*
> *I deeply and completely love and accept myself*

> *Tap while you watch and feel the story unfold.*
> *Tap on the worst parts.*
> *Tap on all the aspects.*

> Note what has changed after you tap

PUTTING IT ALL BEHIND YOU - IN THE P.A.S.S.T. !!

Am I feeling Pain?

Tap on the pain.
Chase the pain if it moves through your body.

Am I Angry?

Tap on the anger.

Am I Sad?

Tap on the sadness.

Am I Stressed?

Tap on the stress

Is there Trauma connected with this?

Tap on the trauma

Celebrate **your sensitivity!**

Use EFT to enhance, expand, enlarge and deepen your gifts!

Problems into Preferences

Let's start with that tapping list that framed all the problems we experience from our sensitivity, and RE-frame them as our gifts. Then we can make them even better!

Now, the following words are mine. You find better ones, ones that fit you and feel good to *you*! Maybe you like to speak in superlatives - use those. Maybe you have better, more profound or more spiritual ways of expressing what is truly the best and loveliest and greatest about you – go for it! Use your best words - ones that make you light up inside!

Tap using the normal EFT spots -
*Instead of saying Even though, say
Especially because...*

~~... I worry that I am TOO sensitive~~
... I LOVE that I am so sensitive... *I choose* to deepen and expand my sensitivity in powerful wonderful ways.

~~I feel so deeply~~
I have this fabulous capacity to feel deeply... *I choose* to accept it as an honor, and learn how to share what I know in ways that are helpful.

THIS IS WHERE I STAND

~~I am so open to others' emotions~~
I have the gift of being able to know people deeply, to even know beyond who they are behind the masks that they use to protect themselves … *I choose* to connect with what is best in them, and stay steady with that, so they can come to see the beauty in themselves as well. And *I choose* to protect myself from their negativity. It just bounces off and away from me.

~~I am easily hurt and upset~~
I am exquisitely sensitive to my own tender feelings, and I acknowledge and honor my feelings for letting me know when I am leaving my center… *I choose* to be surprised to remember more and more times when I was able to hear something upsetting and maintain a sense of my own truth.

~~I don't like conflict~~
I have a deep appreciation for harmony and unity… *I choose* to be even more surprised and delighted to discover how many times a day I can feel it. I know the more I am aware of my own deep harmony, the more harmony there is in the world.

~~It's is hard to stop feeling sad sometimes~~
I know I have the ability to hold on to a feeling by talking to myself about the situation… *I choose* to discover how many things I can find to say about myself that are positive, and that make me happy.

~~I can't watch the news or sad or violent movies~~
I am very responsive to the stories I hear and see in the media. *I choose* what to give my attention to, so I can fill my world with joy and fun and comfort for me… *I choose* to be fascinated to watch humanity learning and growing, even – or especially from its mistakes.

Profoundly light-hearted strategies for unsticking stuck stuff

THIS IS WHERE I STAND

I choose to trust the flow of the universe, and trust that my awareness of humanity's goodness can flow through even the "bad news."

~~I get depressed easily~~
I feel so deeply about my life and the world…*I choose* to use my strengths and creativity to make a difference right where I am, right now.

~~I get overwhelmed~~
~~I can't stand large crowds~~
~~I can't take loud noise~~
~~I don't like hectic environments~~
~~I wish I were tougher and could let things roll off easier~~
I do my best to take good care of myself… *I choose* to find even better and more effective ways to let myself know that I am the best and most valuable me there is!

~~I think my sensitivity is a weakness~~
I like that I am sensitive… *I choose* to love and appreciate and honor this powerful, world changing soul quality that I have been so blessed with. The world needs what I have to offer! I am ready to be more!

~~I think something is wrong with me. It is my fault.~~
I think that I am a good person…*I choose* to open to what I know in my deepest heart that I can become! I love and appreciate and honor this precious being that I am!

~~I wish things didn't bother me so much~~
I am glad that I am so aware …*I choose* to trust the Universe to handle the problems and I use my awareness and my energy to make a difference in this world that I care so much about

~~I wish my emotions weren't so obvious to other people~~
~~I hide my sensitivity from others.~~

People always know what I am feeling,...*I choose* to honor and celebrate who I am, and appreciate that people always know where I stand. *I choose* to stand up and be known for my best and most outstanding ideas.

Continue tapping saying *Especially because*...

...I have this wonderful gift of being able to think and speak in abstract big picture, profound concepts... *I choose* to deepen and strengthen my ability to be an Imagineer, and use my manifestation ability even better so that the goodness I sense has a space to live in in this world.

...being cooperative and diplomatic is important to me ...
I choose to break the rules that aren't working for me and make new ones that feel right, in ways that still honor other peoples' integrity and intentions

...I hunger for deep and meaningful relationships... I make creating and maintaining a good and satisfying relationship with myself my first priority.

...I value personal growth, authenticity and integrity ...
I choose to discover my own strengths and excellence, and do everything I can to enlarge them.

...I am internally deeply caring... *I choose* to take just as good care of myself as I do of _____.

...I am deeply committed to the positive and the good ...
I choose to honor that commitment to myself!

Profoundly light-hearted strategies for unsticking stuck stuff

THIS IS WHERE I STAND

…I have a mission to bring peace to the world… *I choose* a mission of bringing peace into my own life

…I have a strong personal morality… *I choose* to stand even taller in my own strong life!

…I often make extraordinary sacrifices for someone / something I believe in… *I choose* MYSELF!!!!

…I have a good imagination… *I choose* to find amazing ways of bringing magic into my life where there was only misery before! Evolution itself depends on how good I get at this!

…I think I am unusual and unique… *I choose* to stand up for myself and express who I am with love and a light heart. No one can resist that…

I choose to use people like this as my models—

They were sensitive idealists just like me!
THEY UNDERSTAND ME!!!

Homer, Virgin Mary, Hans Christian Andersen, Princess Diana, Gandhi, Shakespeare

NOTES

Profoundly light-hearted strategies for unsticking stuck stuff

The Earth is calling us to this work
A Meditation

Take a moment to relax your hands in your lap and be inside, in whatever way is comfortable and appropriate for you...

Take some deep breaths...

Take a moment to appreciate who you are...
all that you have been in this life...
and continue to be in this life...
with all of these experiences...
in spite of everything...
doing your very best, with great courage, to promote healing in yourself...
and healing in humanity...
and healing on the Earth...

And take a moment to **appreciate** that living your life in this way, with this very focus, is a vitally generative sacred act that calls upon the deepest sovereignty of your being...

It calls upon all your strength, all your love, your largest vision of the future, your most heart-felt trust...
all the best qualities of the best that's in you.

And imagine that the Earth itself has called YOU here, to live this life for exactly this purpose, on behalf of us all; on behalf of the evolution of consciousness.

Your effort and your faith are shaping the future.

.

THIS IS WHERE I STAND

Sense yourself responding to this urgent call.
Knowing that you are doing exactly the right thing, in
exactly the right way...

Even through your pain you are a blessing..

Take a moment to breathe that thought into knowing...

And in a timing that is right for you, open your eyes and
return to this moment...

to this experience that we're all sharing, with as much
gratitude and love as you can muster, even through all the
pain, for this world that so gracefully holds us all.

Thanks to all of us.

Thank you.

Poet David Whyte grew up among the hills
and valleys of Yorkshire, England... he is one of the few poets to take his perspectives on creativity into the field of organizational development, where he works with many American and international companies. He holds a degree in Marine Zoology, and has traveled extensively, including working as a naturalist guide and leading anthropological and natural history expeditions. He brings this wealth of experiences to his poetry, lectures and workshops.

In organizational settings, using poetry and thoughtful commentary, he illustrates how we can foster qualities of courage and engagement; qualities needed if we are to respond to today's call for increased creativity and adaptability in the workplace.

In addition to his five volumes of poetry, David Whyte is the author of *The Heart Aroused: Poetry* and *the Preservation of the Soul in Corporate America*, published by Doubleday / Currency, *Crossing the Unknown Sea: Work as a Pilgrimage of Identity*, published by Riverhead Books, an audio lecture series and an album of poetry and music. He lives with his family in the Pacific Northwest.

Many Rivers Press 1992 • ManyRiversPress.com

Dr. Elaine Aron is the bestselling author of *The Highly Sensitive Person* and its companion books, *The Highly Sensitive Person's Workbook*, *The Highly Sensitive Person in Love* and *The Highly Sensitive Child*. Material in this book reprinted with permission from Dr. Elaine Aron. This material comes from HSPperson.com.

Mary Oliver is the author of several volumes of poetry, including *Why I Wake Early*; *Owls and Other Fantasies: Poems and Essays*; *Winter Hours: Prose, Prose Poems, and Poems*; *West Wind*; *White Pine*; *New and Selected Poems*, which won the National Book award; House of Light, which won the Christopher Award and the L. L. Winship/PEN New England Award; and American Primitive, for which she won the Pulitzer Prize.

The first part of her book-length poem *The Leaf and the Cloud* was selected for inclusion in *The Best American Poetry 1999* and the second part, "*Work*," will be in *The Best American Poetry 2000*. Her books of prose include *Long Life: Essays and Other Writings*; *Rules for the Dance: A Handbook for Writing and Reading Metrical Verse*; *Blue Pastures*; and *A Poetry Handbook*.

Her honors include an American Academy of Arts & Letters Award, a Lannan Literary Award, the Poetry Society of America's Shelley Memorial Prize and Alice Fay di Castagnola Award, and fellowships from the Guggenheim Foundation and the National Endowment for the Arts. Mary Oliver holds the Catharine Osgood Foster Chair for Distinguished Teaching at Bennington College, and lives in Provincetown, Massachusetts, and Bennington, Vermont. This info from Poets.org

Dr. Kyra Mesich, PsyD., is the

author of *The Sensitive Person's Survival Guide*. She has a holistic psychotherapy practice in St Paul, MN in which she specializes in helping sensitive adults and children.

Dr. Mesich's work has focused on natural remedies for sensitive people. Material in this book reprinted with permission from Dr. Kyra Mesich. KyraMesich.com.

Alison Luterman was raised in New England, but

moved to Oakland, California in 1990. Since that time she has worked as an HIV counselor, a drug and alcohol counselor, a drama teacher and a freelance reporter and has taught a number of poetry workshops in schools.

As a writer she is known as a poet, essayist, short story writer and playwright. Her pieces have appeared in publications *Poetry East, Poet Lore, Whetstone, Kalliope, Oberon, The Sun, Kshanti, The Brooklyn Review, Poet Lore, Kalliope.*

She describes her poetry as "accessible... with a spiritual focus, grounded in the real world of my daily life". Her first book, *The Largest Possible Life* won the Cleveland State University Poetry Prize 2000 and was published in 2001. She also says that: "My strength as a writer comes from my willingness to be naked and vulnerable, and to connect my own small set of concerns to the larger questions and concerns of humanity."

See more poems here:
oldpoetry.com/authors/Alison%20Luterman and plagiarist.com/poetry/4391/

Invisible Work (p 117) is from *The Largest Possible Life*
Cleveland State Univ Poetry Center (March 30, 2001)
This poem was originally published in *The Sun* magazine.

David Spangler is a husband, the
father of four children, a warm-hearted and thoughtful
writer, philosopher and teacher of spiritual perspectives.
He has given permission to use his words in this book.

You can learn more at lorian.org, where you will find
this introduction to his work:

"Incarnational Spirituality is the foundation for all of Lorian's work. It
is an affirmation of the spirit innate within our world, our humanity,
our physicality, and our personal lives. It sees each person as a source of
spiritual power and radiance.

Incarnational Spirituality brings a holistic perspective to spirituality.
The spiritual life is often seen as focusing upon the transpersonal and
the transcendent, directing our attention beyond the world and beyond
the self. Incarnational Spirituality seeks to balance this by restoring an
awareness of the spiritual nature of our physical, everyday selves and the
sacredness of the world around us.

Incarnational Spirituality is grounded in our sovereignty as individuals.
Each of us is a unique incarnation of sacredness able to make contributions
that no one else can make to the wellbeing of our world and the positive
unfoldment of our future.

Incarnational Spirituality is a calling to discover the nobility and spiritual
presence in our everyday selves. It is a calling to unfold capacities of blessing,
manifesting, creating, and healing within us.

Incarnational Spirituality is a calling of responsibility to each other and to
our world. It is a calling to act and not just reflect, to engage and not just
contemplate. How a person answers that calling is up to him or her. We
each serve in unique ways. Incarnational Spirituality can offer tools that
assist us in doing so, demonstrating the unity of inner alignment with
outer activity."

THIS IS WHERE I STAND

 **William Elliott**, International traveler, adventurer, author, lecturer and golfer, has spent many years asking extraordinary people profound and meaningful questions.

In his first book, the best seller, *Tying Rocks to Clouds,* he traveled the world interviewing a number of the world's renowned spiritual leaders and greatest thinkers, including the Dalai Lama and Mother Teresa.

A Place at the Table, his most recent work, is a chronicle of Elliott's quest to understand Jesus. He interweaves his own personal, often quirky, epiphanies with insights of well-known men and women of every spiritual tradition - from Deepak Chopra and Marianne Williamson to Mother Teresa and Billy Graham.

His books are a combination reportage and memoir; both intensely personal and universally appealing.

from WilliamElliott.com

Deborah Mitnik: I used to be a "conventional" therapist.

I was "good," but I never truly saw anyone get totally over a trauma or a phobia. I saw my clients learn better how to cope with their problems, but not totally overcome them.

I received excellent and formal training from a psychoanalytic institute and I truly believed that the method I learned was the best method.

So, when I began to learn some of the newer, more innovative methods of trauma and phobia reduction or resolution, such as Emotional Freedom Techniques (EFT), and Traumatic Incident Reduction (TIR), I was very skeptical! They seemed "too easy" because people didn't have to be in therapy for years. They seemed too "hocus pocus" because they involved "tapping" on the face, or rolling the eyes and humming, or repeatedly telling about the trauma in a session longer than the conventional 50 minutes.

How did I get over my skepticism? Personal Experience! I did a couple of sessions of TIR and EFT on myself. My first TIR session took just 90 minutes. A memory that had "run" my life since I was three years old just disappeared!

read more at: trauma-tir.com

Nancy Selfridge, M.D.

Chief, Complementary Medicine Center
Group Health Cooperative
Madison, Wisconsin

"I have been practicing family medicine for about 20 years. I suffered from fibromyalgia for over 20 years and always believed that there was a way to get free of the debilitating pain of this disorder. A few years ago, I was introduced to the mind-body work of Dr. John Sarno. I developed a protocol for applying his principles to my own pain, and I have been free of symptoms ever since.

"In 2003 I co-authored a book, FREEDOM FROM FIBROMYALGIA, with a patient who also got "cured," detailing the methods we used to accomplish this. These tools, coupled with mind-body techniques like meditation and adding now the EFT that Rue teaches , show great promise in helping people with the chronic pain that so often fails to respond to traditional medical treatment."

Nancy is an avid bicyclist, routinely riding 90 miles on a weekend day. Two or three times a year she leads a bike tour in the mountains of Italy. She also contributes much of her time and talent with a local theater troupe putting her creative talents to use designing costumes, acting, writing, singing and doing stand-up comedy.

She has been outspoken about the mis-information spread by the pharmaceutical industry. When complimented by a local newspaper for being willing to take a stand, she said,"It literally makes me sick to compromise. I can't. Taking a stand is the only way I can be well."

Rue Anne Hass, M.A.

Master EFT Practitioner

I have been in private practice as an intuitive mentor/ life path coach in Madison, Wisconsin since 1986 using what I think of as "profoundly lighthearted strategies for unsticking stuck stuff."

A long time ago, I was a college English teacher. From being a teacher I learned about how to learn, how to think about what was important, and how to communicate that clearly. I also learned that people in positions of authority are given respect whether they deserve it or not, and I set an intention for myself to deserve the respect I was given.

This was in the 1960's and early 70's, a time of a great creative ferment in the US and the world. I found myself in the center of this paradigm shift, deeply involved in the women's movement and the anti-war movement, living in an urban commune in Chicago that shared income, child care and household tasks. My job in our group was to take care of the household automobiles. (I was also teaching auto mechanics in a women's educational cooperative). From the experiences of this time I learned a sense of agency: that I had a place in the world, that we are all part of a bigger picture, that what I did and thought mattered.

For seven years, from 1974-1981, I was a staff member of the Findhorn Foundation, an international center for spiritual and holistic education in Scotland. Here, I was deeply challenged to learn and experience my own spiritual truth, independent of spiritual teachers and what other people said were the prerequisites for spiritual progress. I learned to surrender my prickly anger and the sense of personal "power over" in order to open to love and "power with".

Since then, I credit much of what I have learned in life to the bright enchantments and difficult challenges of motherhood and marriage. My daughters are now in their 20's, beautiful young women from the inside out. I am profoundly honored that they set me up with their

their friends for counseling/coaching sessions when I visit them. One is an acupuncturist in Denver, Colorado, and the other is in marketing in Boston, Massachusetts. I married Timothy at Findhorn. He works for an outpatient psychiatric unit, plays soccer, and would meditate all day if somebody paid him to. I think of him as a "mystic jock."

Over the years I have sought out extensive training in psycho-spiritual philosophy and therapies. Today, EFT is the centerpiece of my work. In January, 2006 I was honored to be named the 14th EFT Master. I love the simplicity and effectiveness of EFT, and the fact that it is a tool that people can take home with them. They don't always have to be going to the "expert" to get "fixed" because they are "broken." Now we have healing at our own fingertips!

What really powers me in my life is an intense curiosity about consciousness and a deep love of the world. I think of myself as a "Wise Woman in Training." (I have no intention of graduating! I will always be in training.)

In a first meeting with a new client/co-creative partner, I might walk them through an interesting process of understanding their life as a story, that I describe as "mapping the history of your future." It concludes with asking you to consider: "What do you want your life to leave in the world as a legacy. How do you want the world to be a better place for your having been here?"

I ask myself this question. What emerges for me is fostering in every way I can imagine, at all times, to my best ability, the concept of "Wealthbeing." This term popped into my head one day when I was thinking about the process of manifestation. To me, Wealthbeing means an interesting synthesis of "well-being" and "being (instead of having) wealth." I want to invite and assist people and communities to move into a sense of the real transformative power of their Wealthbeing, their own specific spiritual Presence in the world.

THIS IS WHERE I STAND

If you read this book, you can probably tell that I am inspired by the work of David Spangler (Everyday Miracles; Parent as Mystic/Mystic as Parent; Blessing: the Art and Practice):

" ....each of us is a collaborative participant in the unfoldment and co-creation of the world. We are each direct links between the primal creative act – the Word from which all things spring – and the world in which we live our daily lives.

We are embodiments of that Word and we speak it in our own unique ways through our lives.

This speaking of the creative Word is the essence of a new emerging 'incarnational spirituality.' We can experience the empowerment of spirituality as support for our ordinary lives, integrating us into the world, based on the sacred in the personal rather than only the transpersonal."

Profoundly light-hearted strategies for unsticking stuck stuff

Angela Treat Lyon

Artist, Author, Success Coach, EFT Trainer, Radio
Show Host

Angela is a pretty radical gal who loves to see people
take hold of their lives and run for all they're worth into
a glorious play of success, health and wealth - that gets
better and better and better for as long as they live. Her
Success Coaching clients take the ball and run so far sometimes she get
hoarse screaming encouragement and inspiration.

After many hard years of embodying the role of the proverbial broke
artist, Angela decided to learn a little about this thing called money, and
how to use it properly. She found that she had lived from deep inside
unsupportive emotions, thoughts and actions since early childhood. When
she changed those to supportive, her life and finances shifted radically.
Immediately. Angela is commited now to helping people learn all they can
about their own mind and what it can do, how they can feel, and what
kind of amazing prosperity they can create once they see what it's all
about. Now she helps people create and live a more fabulous life than they
ever thought was possible. Much better than being a reclusive, broke (and
broken) artist!

Angela found Rue's website in 2002, and says, "I instantly liked Rue - just
from her photo. She seemed like someone with whom I could have a really
good, deep conversation, and who would 'get' some of the ideas I have
that most people roll their eyes at. I invited her to do some teleclasses
through my Wealth-Building site, PIGEES.com, and we liked doing it as a
team so much that we have produced a whole series of calls and booklets
- and we started collaborating on longer books. This
is our first one, and there will be more in the future. She writes, I edit,
design and build the book. Good combo. Good fun!"

You will find a whole bunch of sites nested and ready to fly at
AngelaTreatLyon.com. Including IDareYouRadio.com.

Profoundly light-hearted strategies for unsticking stuck stuff

THIS IS WHERE I STAND
by © Rue Hass 2005
protected by International Copyright Laws

Rue@IntuitiveMentoring.com

All illustrations
© Angela Treat Lyon 1996-2005
Cover design, editing, book design and construction
by Angela Treat Lyon

Rue@IntuitiveMentoring.com

Printed in the United States
211265BV00007B/12/P